Speaking of Jesus

Speaking of Jesus

Finding the Words for Witness

RICHARD LISCHER

F FORTRESS PRESS   PHILADELPHIA

Library of Congress Cataloging in Publication Data

Lischer, Richard.
Speaking of Jesus.

1. Evangelistic work. I Title.
BV3790.L47   248'.5   81-70556
ISBN 0–8006–1631–6 (pbk.)   AACR2

9396J81   Printed in the United States of America   1–1631

To Bill and Barbara Wagner
friends and partners in the gospel

Contents

Preface

THE WORD *laity* is derived from the Greek word *laos*, which is most commonly translated "people." When I say that this book is for laypeople, I am thinking of the New Testament's *laos tou theou*—the people of God. Evangelism belongs to them (us), as should most books about evangelism. By claiming a lay audience, I do not mean to imply that professional ministers have greater skills in communicating the gospel and therefore will not benefit from these pages, but only that whoever reads this book will not find in it the technical language of theology.

The terms *evangelism, witness, communication of the gospel,* and several others all have special shades of meaning, and in different places I have taken note of these nuances. But for the most part they are used interchangeably to describe the transmission of the message of God's love in Christ from one person to another, to the end that those who do not know Christ might believe in him and do his will. Or, from another perspective, that those who live on the margins of the church might be incorporated into Christ's body and there find integration and wholeness.

The most neglected feature of contemporary evangelism is the church. It is either dismissed as an irrelevancy by the electronic evangelists or trivialized into membership statistics by the mainline denominations. In either case the fullness of its life in the Lord is unappreciated. It will not be difficult to detect this book's congregational bias. I write not only out of my experience in several diverse congregations, but also out of the conviction that the *laos tou theou,* the people of God, may be found in its fullness when gathered into communities around Word and sacrament.

Evangelism *is* the community itself radiating light and warmth from an energy source hidden deep within its midst. Do not be misled by this word *congregation* or imagine that I have only one kind of social formation in mind when I use it. I offer only the atoms: Word, sacraments, Spirit, Lord, people. Readers may assemble the molecule as they see fit.

With this book I begin to discharge my debt to one congregation, Prince of Peace Lutheran Church in Virginia Beach, Virginia, whose evangelists first studied this material in mimeographed worksheets and then put it to work in their personal lives. More than anything else, their encouraging response has enabled me to keep on with this study even after our partnership in witness had come to an end. Here at Duke I wish to thank my colleague Kelly Ingram for bibliographical suggestions and Candice Yeary Sloan for her supervision of the typing and retyping of the manuscript.

The Divinity School   RICHARD LISCHER
Duke University
Durham, North Carolina

CHAPTER ONE
The Charge

What I tell you in the dark, utter in the light; and what you hear whispered, proclaim upon the housetops.

Matt. 10:27

It was inevitable that any religion whose central message was called "good news" would be a missionary movement. And so it was from the beginning. From Galilee to Rome, a distance of 1,500 miles and innumerable cultures, the Christian message was spread by word of mouth, people telling other people about Jesus of Nazareth. In an era that is militantly protective of the individual's right to privacy and among churches increasingly ashamed of evangelism because of its hard-sell associations, it seems necessary to reaffirm the obvious: Christianity is a missionary movement. Christians have been commissioned to speak about Jesus.

THE FIRE

The good news about Jesus Christ comes fully alive only in its expression between persons. Words precede thought. Primitive humans did not ruminate on the concept of the flint for months or millennia before saying, "This is a flint." But as they shaped it or struck it they said, "Now *that's* a flint!" Early Christians did not meditate on the notion of good news for even the slightest period of time before shaping it to the lips of ordinary people and striking it against the hard edge of a pagan environment. In the shaping and striking, the Word became good news to both teller and hearer. The result was fire.

1

If we are to be revisited by the fire, we will need to recover the centrality of bringing Jesus Christ to conscious articulation for the sake of others. No group or denomination of Christians willfully places itself outside the original tradition of the church. Each denomination operates according to its own kind of genetic code within which, if it is not careful, it may become hopelessly trapped. The code contains each body's link with the central tradition of the church. For fundamentalists, it is the five fundamental doctrines; for Pentecostalists, it is tangible experience of the Holy Spirit; for many Protestants, it is the enculturation of the personal and social ethics of the New Testament; for Episcopalians, it is the transmission of the ordained ministry; for Roman Catholics, it is the authority of Rome. Admittedly, these are caricatures of the churches, but caricatures drawn to this point: if the transmission of the good news to nonbelievers is not present in the church's code, no matter how vocally it celebrates its links to real Christianity, it lies outside the originating tradition. And its members (the addressees of this book) are therefore deprived and shielded from authentic participation in the historic movement called Christianity.

At its earliest stages the movement never envisioned the kind of evangelism promotions mounted by twentieth-century churches. Despite the millions of dollars American churches have poured into saturation evangelism efforts, the primitive church was more effective than we in communicating Christ. Jesus sent eleven people into an empire of two hundred seventy million, and within one hundred fifty years of that commission one of the greatest of the Latin church fathers, Tertullian, was able to taunt the Roman emperor with the words:

> We are but of yesterday, yet we have filled every place among you—cities, islands, fortresses, towns, marketplaces, camp, tribes, town councils, the palace, the senate, the forum; we have left nothing to you but the temples of your gods.[1]

While we are not sure *how* the primitive, post-New Testament era church carried out its mission, Tertullian makes it clear that the gospel had caught hold and was burning out of control. The manner of its spread has been a question of scholarly debate. Was it an orderly transmission of a message painstakingly memorized and repeated according to the model of rabbinic education? Or did the church grow by means of a series of pneumatic explosions as community after community caught fire with the Holy Spirit? Did the movement thrive originally on the transmission of relatively simple proclamations, such as "Jesus is Lord!" and "Christ is risen!"? Or did early Christians form themselves into communities of teachers and storytellers? What was Christian worship like? And what role did it play in the spreading of the gospel? This book does not intend to answer all of these questions and more for their own sakes. Whatever the form of its evangelism, the Christian movement was always *there,* striking against the edge of something that was *not* grace, redemption, love, kingdom, or heaven. It had not yet bought into the swamp that measures a church's commitment to society by its willingness to imitate society; nor had it yet been chewed up and spit out as a "general Christian influence" on Western culture. The primitive church recognized something apart from and different from itself and addressed this.

Any definition of evangelism must maintain the gospel's otherness; otherwise there is no good *(eu)* message *(angelion),* no *gut Spiel* or *godspel,* to offer those without it. Alarmed at the secularism in its midst, the contemporary church has begun to redefine or replace evangelism with education, catechesis, or other forms of Christian nurture in an effort to convert those who already identify themselves with the church. The maintenance and spiritual development of Christians is a laudable concern and one that rightly takes place in the midst of the Christian community's worship and fellowship. But it cannot replace the effort that goes on outside the circle. In its preoccupation with people who need to grow, the church cannot turn its back on those who have not been born.

Nowadays evangelism is more likely to be associated with mass movements or ecclesiastical policies spearheaded by highly visible evangelistic preachers or highly invisible church bureaucrats and planners. In any case, while these are valid expressions of evangelism, they do not touch on the matter of this book, which will not deal with ecclesiastical policies for recouping losses nor with congregational strategies for growing big churches. This evangelism "from above" threatens to take the work away from those who had it from the beginning—the people of God.

I shall seek to describe and advocate the transmission of the gospel at the grass-roots level of the church. Given the reality that most Christians are not television superstars or denominational policymakers, how may rank-and-file Christians participate in the ongoing witness to the gospel? It has always been relatively easy to see how the church's most visible leaders transmit the message. We know how Billy Graham practices evangelism, but centuries from now will historians interpret his crusades as the norm for Christian communication? We have read about the camp meetings and revivals of the Great Awakening, but what *else* was going on from day to day? From the ancient church we have the legacy of second-century writers, the Apologists, whose literary witness remains as a monument to their faith and intelligence. We know how the philosopher Justin Martyr argued for the faith, but of the informal sharing, telling, and testifying sustained by ordinary Christians in the daily routine, we know practically nothing. The pagan Celsus gives only a clue when he complains of evangelism carried on in "private houses" by "workers in wool and leather, laundry workers and the most illiterate and bucolic yokels."[2] That it was a people's movement we can be sure, but in the words of historian Michael Green, "one would give a lot to know how the man in the street was won to Christ in antiquity."[3] It is precisely at the street level, however, where the church, *our* church, will win or lose the battle of evangelism.

I offer this book to those who live the Christian witness in the schools they attend, in the places where they work, and in the neighborhoods where they live. It is for those who still believe or are ready to be convinced that the Word of God flowers most beautifully in spontaneous, interpersonal relationships. Everyone knows that evangelism works through acts of love and faithfulness as well as through words. Those actions may be as personal as the gift of hot soup to an ailing neighbor or as impersonal as a

church's budgetary allocation for world hunger. This book, however, will be about the words—and especially the *stories*—that
Christians speak to non-Christians in order to call forth repentance, faith, and discipleship. The remainder of this chapter will
outline the commission to spread the gospel and analyze several
New Testament models of evangelism.

THE SEED

There is no polite or unobtrusive way of reminding evangelists
that the work belongs to God. The glory of evangelism is the fire;
the mystery of evangelism is the seed. Before we are Christian
incendiaries we are Christian farmers or, less than that, awed ob-
servers of the miracle of seed, soil, and growth.

There is a hiddenness in the work God does among us—as obscure as the deity in Jesus of Nazareth, as still as the kingdom he
ushered into Palestine, and as indirect as the stories he told about
the kingdom of his Father.

His parables are metaphors of a mysterious presence that no
one recognizes: of the inscrutable generosity of a vineyard foreman, of the unrecognized goodness of a son killed by spiteful ten-
ants, of hidden treasure, and of a coin misplaced. But most of all
they are stories of seeds: "A sower went out to sow . . ."

Year after year the farmer prepares the land, discs and culti-
vates it, prays over it, and in the good years harvests it. God has
that feeling for the land. God continues to ready the soil for plant-
ing so that the seed, which the Scripture identifies as the Word of
God, can be sown. The sower loves the soil and gives it every
opportunity to be rich and productive. In three years of service
in a country church, I heard many reasons why the crops would
not grow—scorching sun, weeds, bugs, birds, thorns, rocks, cold
weather, and the government—but never any complaints about
the seed. The seed is always good and, if given half a chance, it
will grow.

It will grow in secret. How susceptible the church has been to
the secret-of-success syndrome that promises to cure spiritual
maladies with institutional remedies. What a relief it is to turn
from the frenzy of "How to Make Your Church Grow" to the

promise of Jesus. "The ground produces a crop by itself, first the blade, then the ear, then full-grown corn in the ear" (Mark 4:28, NEB). The Greek word for "by itself" is a familiar one to Western ears: *automatē*. But far from reflecting the automatic performance of human technologies, it suggests the providential ordering recognized by the writer of Ecclesiastes:

> A generation goes, and a generation comes,
>   but the earth remains for ever.
> The sun rises and the sun goes down,
>   and hastens to the place where it rises. (1:4–5)

That Jesus extends the image of natural growth to God's rule in the world is of great comfort to all evangelists. It also punctures our pretensions. All the nervous energy of the church cannot make the kingdom come. We participate in its coming, but not as agents. This is why Paul wrote to his congregation, "I planted, Apollos watered, but God gave the growth" (1 Cor. 3:6). In the midst of religious and political upheaval Martin Luther once said, "While I drink my little glass of Wittenberg beer the gospel runs its course."[4] This is a remarkable confession, for if ever a person worked, plotted, and strove toward a goal, it was Luther. But he realized that at the back of his and all the church's energies is the quiet, miraculous presence of God's rule in the world.

Faith in that presence yields a sense of stillness and serenity. The Bible calls it not peace of mind but the peace of God that passes all understanding. Its characteristic posture is that of attentiveness to God's Word. The Christian who aspires to communicate this gospel of peace will first learn to listen to it and in the listening will find the means of articulation.[5] Thus, not only as a prerequisite for witnessing but also in the very doing of evangelism we listen, wait, learn, grow, and suffer, never disdaining the mystery or the miracle of the seed.

THE COMMISSION

Christians have always considered themselves to be a people under orders. No matter how spontaneously the growth and spread of the good news appears to have taken place, those who participated in the first waves of its expansion did so in obedience to a divine command.

If we listen carefully, we can still hear the charge. It may be the Great Commission of Matt. 28:19: "Go therefore and make disciples of all nations, baptizing them in the name of the Father and of the Son and of the Holy Spirit." But it may not. Depending on our role in the church or our church's relative strength in society, the Great Commission may create in us feelings of inadequacy. For it sounds more like an impersonal edict than a word of the Lord and, though never out of place in a local congregation, seems more appropriate to a church convention or a world evangelism congress.

In the local congregation those who have made an intentional commitment to evangelism do not see themselves as world winners, but as cells or small expeditionary forces. They identify with those lesser commissionings recorded earlier in the Gospels because they, like so many would-be builders of the kingdom, are decidedly less. This is Mark's account:

> And he called to him the twelve, and began to send them out two by two, and gave them authority over the unclean spirits. He charged them to take nothing for their journey except a staff; no bread, no bag, no money in their belts; but to wear sandals and not put on two tunics. And he said to them, "Where you enter a house, stay there until you leave the place. And if any place will not receive you and they refuse to hear you, when you leave, shake off the dust that is on your feet for a testimony against them." (Mark 6:7–11)

For several reasons we hear this lesser commissioning more clearly. First, it proposes a narrower field, a geographical area of more manageable, congregational scope than "the world." This is an expedition anchored to its sender and pledged to return to him. Second, it takes the possibility of rejection seriously. In Mark's account Jesus does not promise that every door will be opened to the disciples, for he knows that they will encounter many who do not give a fig for the kingdom and have given up on the Messiah. When today's church hears its commission, it must also hear in this passage the echo of another church's struggle with the possibility of failure. Third, this commissioning sug-

gests a method. Jesus sends his followers out in six teams of two.
They are sent out in teams not to prevent boredom or to shore up
one another's arguments, but because together they are the
church in mission *(co-missio)*, and the church is never isolated.
Not everyone who speaks of Christ does so with a regular witnessing partner, but no one who communicates the faith does so
in isolation from the church. The church creates and sponsors
partnerships between witnesses so that brothers and sisters in this
enterprise may love one another, pray with and for one another,
suffer together, rejoice together, and bear one another's burdens.

The only ammunition Christian evangelists take with them is
the authority of Christ. In the Gospel accounts these evangelists
go so far as to strip themselves of all preparation, from rehearsed
words to supplies of food and money, so that their reliance may
be on God alone. The need for this methodological nakedness has
to do with the epoch-making nature of the task. This is no ordinary expedition, for the supernatural authority wielded by the
disciples signals the beginning of a new age. It marks the breaking in of God's transcendent authority and the defeat of evil (in
one account, when they return Jesus cries, "I saw Satan fall . . ."
Luke 10:18). Contemporary witnesses must remember that they
participate in this new order. The commission is the same, the
work is the same, and the Christ is the same. The proclamation
of the kingdom continues as a sign of this aeon's change of age.
Today's messengers of the kingdom are both the historical succes-
sors of the apostles and their contemporaries in the kingdom,
which, after twenty centuries, remains hidden in our midst.

CHRIST THE COMMUNICATOR

Christ's death and resurrection ignited the church's witness and
continues to fuel it in the present day. From the perspective of
that transforming event it is now possible for Christians to listen
in on that power at work in ordinary conversations and to hear
echoes of the earliest church's missionary strategy. The portrait
of Jesus in the Gospels reveals a pattern of communication that
continues to instruct and inspire his witnessing church.

First, his pattern of communication was *dialogic;* he listened and entered fully into the world of the seeker. Jesus never used the questions of his dialogue partners as springboards for his premeditated answers but as a means of probing the heart. To Jesus the shape and intent of the question mattered. When a man approached him with the salutation, "Good Teacher," before the man's religious question was answered, Jesus turned his salutation back on him: "Why do you call me good?" (Mark 10:17–18). So you want to inherit eternal life. Why? How badly? In this case a question about salvation—a religious issue—was quickly translated into a probing analysis of the man's motives and priorities. Through dialogue the man (known to us as "the rich young ruler") *participated* in this analysis of his spiritual motives and, as Mark tells us, "went away sorrowful; for he had great possessions." Likewise in speaking with Nathanael, Jesus is not content to receive Nathanael's confession, "Rabbi, you are the Son of God! You are the King of Israel!" without helping Nathanael understand why and on what grounds he blurted out his confession (John 1:49–50). Jesus' use of the dialogic method always led beyond self-discovery to the decisive issues of God and his kingdom.

Second, Jesus' way of communicating good news was *holistic.* He approached human beings as integrated, whole persons and did not observe our nice distinctions between body and spirit, life and heart, suffering and sin, health and salvation, hospital and chapel, food and Bible passages. He forgave the sick and healed the sinners! When confronted with a paralytic, Jesus had the audacity to say, "Take heart, my son; your sins are forgiven." Then, as confirmation of that authority to forgive, Jesus healed the man's bodily ailment. In Jesus there was never a discrepancy between word and deed. Forgiveness was never isolated from physical wholeness or social reintegration. His holistic ministry embodied the psalmist's words,

> Bless the Lord, O my soul,
>   and forget not all his benefits,
> who forgives all your iniquity,
>   who heals all your diseases. . . . (Ps. 103:2–3)

Third, Jesus' approach to evangelism was *situational*. That is to say, he went "on location" with the gospel. In Jesus' pursuit of sinners we see one of the great differences between him and other notable rabbis. The rabbis would *allow* a penitent sinner to come into their midst, but no one had ever gone into the streets to seek out sinners as Jesus had. He found Matthew in the tax office, the Samaritan woman at the well drawing water, Zacchaeus dangling from a sycamore tree, Nicodemus nervously pacing in the temple shadows, Mary at the hearth, Martha in the kitchen, 5,000 in a lonely, inaccessible place. He ate and drank with sinners. He went where the people were—where they worked, played, shopped, and worshiped—and did not insist on moral prerequisites before talking with them. Zacchaeus did not *first* have to give up his thievery, or the Samaritan woman her lover, or Nicodemus his cowardice in order to come into the presence of Jesus. What happened as a result of hearing his good news was another story! Jesus' aggressive, situational approach to evangelism might be answer enough to the church member who says, "They know where the church is. Been there thirty years. Let them come to us."

Fourth, Jesus communicated in *simple* language. In his discussion of the parables, Amos Wilder speaks of the secularity of Jesus' language.[6] He did not maintain a rigid distinction between sacred and secular language in the communication of his good news. Mark tells us "the common people heard Christ gladly"—probably because they could understand him. He spoke the language of their experience: he told about a man who was attacked traveling the treacherous road from Jerusalem to Jericho. He communicated his understanding of the farmer's lot. How *does* one make anything grow in this miserable soil? How does one harvest a wheat field in which a devious neighbor has sowed darnel? "Once upon a time there was an ungrateful boy who wanted to leave home. . . . Let us suppose you have one hundred sheep, and one goes astray. . . . Can you imagine working all day in the heat and receiving the same pay as a laborer who worked one hour?"

Jesus avoided abstract theological language in favor of vivid metaphor: "Foxes have holes, and birds of the air have nests; but the Son of man has nowhere to lay his head." "Follow me, and I will make you fishers of men." "If your right eye causes you to sin, pluck it out and throw it away." "Why do you see the speck that is in your brother's eye, but do not notice the log that is in your own eye?" The basic unit of all metaphor, including extended metaphors (that is, parables), is the *comparison* of unlike entities. The challenge of comparison remains the ongoing task of every evangelist who wishes to portray the reality of God in graspable, human terms: "When I became a Christian it was like ..." "Christ means more to me than ..." "My participation in this church now is as natural as. ..."

Fifth, Jesus' approach to gospel communication was *decisive.* He did not content himself to move among people as a teacher, healer, or miracle worker without calling his listeners to decision. It was this authority which startled people, for he called for an ultimate response to his person. In the last analysis his ideas were subordinated to who he was: "Follow *me,*" he said. Today we hear much about the necessity of a "decision for Christ." Decision *is* important, but it is for the moment. Discipleship is for the long haul. Whenever decision is severed from discipleship the result is what Dietrich Bonhoeffer called "cheap grace." Bonhoeffer's classic definition continues to sting a complacent church: "Cheap grace is the grace we bestow on ourselves ... the preaching of forgiveness without requiring repentance, baptism without church discipline, communion without confession. Cheap grace is grace without discipleship."[7] Some approaches to evangelism strive only to maintain a "presence" in a secular world; others are content to announce the Word, often by means of electronic images or mass rallies, without becoming involved in those relationships which nurture growth and discipleship. These approaches fall short of New Testament standards, for Jesus moved among people to effect the decisive change known as repentance and the permanent process known as discipleship.

NEW TESTAMENT MODELS

Witness. The great Ceylonese theologian D. T. Niles once wrote, "Evangelism is witness. It is one beggar telling another beggar

where to get food."[8] The difference between evangelism and witnessing is that evangelism tells *the* story and witnessing tells *my*
part in that story. In the language of the courtroom, the witness
tells what he or she saw or heard, not with uninvolved or dispassionate objectivity, but from a particular, personal perspective.
"Witnessing" has a contagious, autobiographical quality: "for we
cannot but speak of what we have seen and heard" (Acts 4:20).
"Go home to your friends, and tell them how much the Lord has
done for you . . ." (Mark 5:19).

Perhaps you have noticed that *witness* is both a verb and a
noun. It is something you do and someone you are. The Greek
root for witness is *martyreo*. In the book of Revelation and in the
years immediately following the New Testament era, *martyreo*
took on the meaning we have associated with *martyr*, one whose
witness includes the shedding of blood and the sacrifice of life.
Those who witnessed in this way were termed Christian "athletes." It is significant that the first postbiblical athlete was not a
strong and attractive youth but an eighty-six-year-old man named
Polycarp. When we think of the martyrs, we think of old Polycarp who, when asked to curse Christ or die, replied, "Eighty-six
years I have served him, and he never did me any wrong. How
can I blaspheme my King who saved me?"[9] Or we think of Dietrich Bonhoeffer sitting in his Nazi prison cell conducting Bible
classes for inmates and guards and writing a poem to God on the
day he was hanged. We think of Archbishop Oscar Romero and
the many Latin American Christians, clerical and lay, who have
witnessed with their lives to violent extremism and the oppression of the poor.

Does the exhortation to testify before the authorities have any
relevance in a democratic society where everyone is free to believe and worship? Is martyrdom possible for us? Perhaps not.
But there are "little martyrdoms" that occur whenever one risks
ridicule, ostracism, or the disruption of a comfortable relationship
because of the compelling call to bear witness. Like the prophets,
John the Baptist, and Jesus himself, authentic witnesses always
find themselves slightly out of sync with society, articulating

words no one wants to hear, engaging in acts of faithfulness no one understands.

There is a touching example of one of these "little martyrdoms" in the quarters of the imperial page boys in the Palatine Hill in Rome. Coming to us from the third century is a drawing, done in a childish hand, entitled "Alexamenos worships his God." It depicts a boy standing before the cross in an attitude of prayer. The figure on the cross is that of a man with an ass's head. One of the pages, a boy named Alexamenos, was a Christian and, in the cruel taunts of his fellow pages, was paying the price for it. Another inscription nearby, perhaps written by a classmate or by Alexamenos himself, reads "Alexamenos is faithful."[10]

Proclaim. This English word summarizes two scriptural phrases which have become synonymous: "proclaim as a herald" and "preach the gospel." The herald proclaims the good news of the coming of the Lord, entering the town in advance of the king and trumpeting his imminent arrival. While the herald personally has little authority, the herald's message nevertheless demands a response. "Today, when you hear his voice, do not harden your hearts" (Heb. 4:7). The term *preach* unfortunately has the distasteful connotation recorded in *Webster's Third International Dictionary:* "to exhort in an officious and tiresome manner." "Don't *preach* at me," we say. However, it also suggests the image of one speaker addressing and exhorting an assembly of listeners. In the Greek language, "preach the good news" is rendered by a single verb which may be literally translated "gospelize." It is not a tiresome harangue, but the articulation and offer of God's love in Christ. *All* Christians are called to preach, to bring this gospel to every situation in which they find themselves. Since I am a preacher, my wife and children have been preached to from a variety of pulpits. But the most important preaching I can do for them and they for me occurs around the kitchen table and in the quiet times we spend together. That's when we "gospelize." It is important to note that the biblical model for preaching focuses not only on the public worship serv-

ices but also upon those one-to-one encounters in which the life
of God in Jesus Christ is offered, shared, and celebrated (see, for
example, Acts 8:35).

Teach. The early church's evangelism was by no means limited
to preaching or the nonrational outbursts of Spirit-filled prophets.
It included intellectual argument and closely reasoned evalua-
tions of scriptural evidence. Without an adequate intellectual basis, Christianity would not have long survived in the Greco-
Roman milieu.[11] Our generation has seen the pendulum swing
away from an emphasis on serious teaching as a form of evangelism toward other, less structured approaches to the development
of faith. For too long the church has approached its teaching in
the quantitative spirit satirized by Mark Twain in *The Adventures of Tom Sawyer.* Through a series of shrewd trades Tom is
able to acquire the tickets issued by his Sunday school to those
who have mastered 2,000 Bible memory texts. When he steps up
to receive his ill-gotten Doré Bible, however, the superintendent
asks if he knows the names of the first two disciples of Jesus, to
which Tom gamely replies, "David and Goliath."

The church has defeated its own purpose by segregating
preaching from teaching. When Jesus commanded his followers to
teach others to observe his commands (Matt. 28:20), he did not
have in mind the pouring of biblical data into empty little (or big)
heads. Biblical literacy is a necessary tool for Christian persua-
sion; we live in and love the sacred texts. But we do not teach the
data for their own sakes. We teach *for* the transformation of life
by the power of the gospel as it is revealed in the Bible. When
Jesus interpreted the Scriptures for his discouraged followers on
the road to Emmaus, or when Paul argued from scriptural evidence concerning Jesus (for example, Acts 17), they were doing
more than offering courses in Old Testament appreciation. They
were teaching for transformation.

The perfect model for the integration of teaching and preaching occurs in Philip's instruction of the Ethiopian eunuch (Acts
8:26–40). When he finds a man who is struggling with the meaning of a Bible text, Philip uses it as a teaching tool to lead the

man to Christ. Philip asks, "Do you understand what you are reading?" And the man answers, "How can I, unless some one guides me?" Philip's teaching ministry includes the patient, verse-by-verse explanation and interpretation of Isaiah 53, a standard procedure for any teacher, but culminates in the telling of the gospel of Jesus (the Greek says "he gospelized him"). The episode climaxes in the question every Christian evangelist prays to hear more often, "What is to prevent my being baptized?"

Invite. America is a nation of joiners. A gregarious people, we belong to legions of clubs and organizations from the Exalted Order of the Moose to the PTA. If it moves, we'll join it. Somewhere along this organizational spectrum lie 340,000 congregations—the "churches"—who also wish to gain members and grow like other organizations. Thus to allow *invitation* as a valid model for evangelism may suggest a blunting of Christian responsibilities and a cheapening of God's grace. What? Invite my neighbor to join another organization? If we invite others *only* to affiliate with our club, we do a disservice to our neighbors and dishonor our call. There is a biblical sense of invitation, however, in which one person invites or brings another into the presence of God and God does the rest. When my children steadfastly refuse to try the heart of the artichoke, as though I were trying to poison them, I know that I cannot force them to enjoy this or other delicacies foreign to their palate. But if I can induce them to try one bite, the artichoke will do the rest. "O taste and see, how gracious the Lord is!"

What does it mean to bring someone to the presence of Jesus? Initially, it may mean to invite the neighbor into the presence of those who honor Christ's name. When Andrew met Jesus, his first task was to introduce his brother, Simon Peter, to the Lord. The next day, after Jesus called Philip, Philip sought his brother Nathanael to tell him of Jesus of Nazareth. When Nathanael replied with the cynical remark, " 'Can anything good come out of Nazareth?' Philip said to him, 'Come and see' " (John 1:35–46). This is to say, "Nothing I can do or say will prove his goodness to you. But I can tell you that when I came to Christ, he changed my life.

When I am open to the Word with other Christians, something new happens to me. Come and see." We cannot persuade one who is freezing to be warm, but we can bring that person to the fire.

Live. A conversation I had with a young man about the Christian faith ended abruptly with the questions, "So what? What's the difference?" Although faith comes by hearing, as Paul says, it is also strengthened by seeing, that is, seeing the difference of the Christian life. If early Christianity had contented itself with an other-worldly message of salvation, it would have survived only in caves, deserts, and citadels of holiness. But the church focused its transcendent power on worldly concerns, such as labor relations, slavery, marriage and the family, the exposure of unwanted newborn babies, cruelty in the amphitheater, and obscenity on the stage.[12] Tertullian's essays are representative of Christianity's this-worldly concerns: *The Crown* (Christian antimilitarism), *On the Spectacles* (the cruelty of the circuses), *Treatises on Marriage and Remarriage.*

The challenge of life witness is already addressed in the New Testament. First Peter speaks to a dilemma that continues to plague relationships, particularly marriages, to this day. Although sexual roles are no longer as rigid as in biblical days, the question framed in 1 Peter is how Christian women, who do not have the freedom to speak of Jesus, might witness to their unbelieving husbands. The author's answer is a surprising one: witness without words. "Likewise you wives, be submissive to your husbands, so that some, though they do not obey the word, may be won without a word by the behavior of their wives, when they see your reverent and chaste behavior" (1 Pet. 3:1–2). The principle here comforts and encourages all Christians living in a non-Christian environment. Christians, choose your words carefully; do not let an obsession with sacred words become an offense! For those who live an explicitly Christian life of worship, prayer, and love, it is possible to make your witness without words. When words have become weapons between you and your spouse, friend, neighbor, or co-worker, there is still something you can do. Your witness has not ceased.

The spirit of that life witness was given classic expression in an anonymous second-century letter to a Roman official named Diognetus. This is the witness of the early church or, more specifically, of one eloquent early Christian to his world and ours:

> Christians cannot be distinguished from the rest of humanity by country or language or customs. They do not separate themselves into cities of their own; they use no special language; nor do they follow an eccentric pattern of life. Their doctrine, unlike that of many religious movements, is not based on human ideas or philosophy. Although they live in Greek and barbarian cities, depending on their place of birth, and follow the usual customs of those cities, they never cease to witness to the reality of another city in which they live. They share in everything as citizens, yet endure everything as aliens. Every foreign land is their fatherland, and yet for them every fatherland is a foreign land.
>
> They marry, like everyone else, and they beget children, but they do not expose their unwanted infants to the elements. They share their board with each other but not their marriage beds.
>
> They busy themselves on earth, but their citizenship is in heaven. They obey the laws of the land but in their own lives go far beyond the laws' requirements. They love all people, and by all people are persecuted. They are put to death, and yet they are brought to life. They are poor, and yet they make many rich; they are completely destitute, and yet they enjoy complete abundance. They are dishonored, and in their dishonor are glorified; they are reviled, and yet they bless. They are treated by the Jews as foreigners and are hunted down by the Greeks; and all the time those who hate them find it impossible to justify their hatred. To put it simply: *What the soul is in the body, that Christians are in the world.*[13]

NOTES

1. *Apology* 37. 4. *The Fathers of the Church*, vol. 10, trans. R. Arbesmann, E. Daly, E. Quain (New York: Fathers of the Church, Inc., 1950), p. 95.

2. Quoted in Michael Green, *Evangelism in the Early Church* (Grand Rapids: Wm. B. Eerdmans Publishing Co., 1970), p. 173.

3. Ibid., p. 161.

4. See Helmut Thielicke, *The Waiting Father*, trans. John W. Doberstein (New York: Harper & Row, 1959), p. 90.

5. See Robert Funk, *Language, Hermeneutic, and Word of God* (New York: Harper & Row, 1966), p. 7.

6. Amos Wilder, *Early Christian Rhetoric* (Cambridge: Harvard University Press, 1964), p. 73.

7. Dietrich Bonhoeffer, *The Cost of Discipleship*, trans. R. H. Fuller (New York: The Macmillan Company, 1959), p. 47.

8. D. T. Niles, *That They May Have Life* (New York: Harper and Brothers, 1951), p. 96.

9. "The Martyrdom of Saint Polycarp," *Early Christian Fathers, The Library of Christian Classics*, vol. 1, trans. and ed. Cyril C. Richardson (Philadelphia: Westminster Press, 1953), p. 152.

10. See Arnold Toynbee, ed., *The Crucible of Christianity* (New York: World Publishing Co., 1969), p. 295. Cf. Green's comments in *Evangelism*, pp. 174–75.

11. See Green's observation in *Evangelism*, p. 160.

12. Ibid., p. 277.

13. "Letter to Diognetus," *Early Christian Fathers, The Library of Christian Classics*, vol. 1, trans. and ed. Cyril C. Richardson (Philadelphia: Westminster Press, 1953), pp. 216–18, slightly paraphrased with italics added.

CHAPTER TWO
The Retreat

And if the bugle gives an indistinct sound, who will get ready for battle?

1 Cor. 14:8

AFTER SIX YEARS of theological education, I undertook a parish ministry in the farmlands of southern Illinois. The congregation to which I was assigned boasted a century-old history of American gothic prosperity and tightknit stability. Because of its isolated location and family composition, the church had not turned its face outward in some time. Mission to its community and neighboring farms, it appeared to me, belonged at the top of the congregation's and my list of priorities. It did not take long for me to discover, however, that the most pressing demand of this new ministry was the one for which I had received the least training and preparation: the communication of the faith from one person to another. I do not refer to preaching, but to something more threatening and difficult than preaching, namely, personal witnessing. A compulsive sense of duty urged me into my car three times a week and drove me over the oil and dirt roads of my parish—to no avail. Despite the best of intentions, the Pinto only stopped at the homes of friends and faithful members. During those long and scenic drives, I had the leisure to develop a rather comprehensive rationale for retreating from the commission with which I and all Christians had been charged. I offer it here, not as a condemnation of either myself or others, but as a realistic attempt to answer the question, Why is it hard for Christians to speak of their faith? Why is it that Christians who cheerfully de-

19

vote hours to boring committee work and institutional drudgery find it impossible to tell others about Christ? At this point it may be helpful for you, the reader, to think about your reasons for not doing the work of evangelism. My guess is that while your reasons may include intellectual misperceptions of evangelism and the usual cultural biases one finds in our society, the cartoon character Pogo's assessment is nearer the truth: "We have met the enemy, and they is us!"

WE HAVE MET THE ENEMY

The retreat from witness comes from within. It begins with a deep-seated ambivalence toward God and God's word. We want to speak, and we do not want to; we want to be known to the other, and we want to hold ourselves in reserve.[1] There is nothing we would like better than to experience honest relationships with others; there is nothing we detest more fiercely than the giving of our precious selves. We are closed fists in a world of closed fists, in a world that desperately needs the open palm.

"If he would only talk to me" is the complaint counselors hear more than any other. "Not about the state of the checking account, the kids' flute lessons, or the daily routine," she continues, "but about himself." I know a young woman who requires professional help for severe bouts with depression. Her parents steadfastly deny her problem and the financial assistance to deal with it. When they berate her about her "moods," they do not tell her about the father's experience of shell shock in World War II and their feelings of shame and fear associated with mental illness. They do not tell the truth because they are afraid of it. The entire family is a tightly clenched fist.

Why must my best kept secret be me? At the center of our very selves is a pocket of unbelief so potent that, like damaged brain tissue, it affects the speech and actions of otherwise healthy Christians. So instead of striding through our lives giving a clear witness to Christ, we limp along making our witness apologetically with halting speech. More is involved in this near-silence than the relative strength or weakness of one's ego. Instinctively we know that words make claims both on hearers and, more threateningly, on speakers. I am somehow implicated in and responsible for the words I speak. If I say "God is love," I have placed the highest value on love and have become responsible for accepting and delivering it.

Meaningful communication is a form of commitment in which two persons risk the revelation of themselves to one another. In human communication there is no authentically personal word without the investment of a person. In the Bible this willingness to risk oneself is symbolized by the telling of one's name. God's commitment to Israel is sealed when God discloses the divine name to Moses. In Christian witnessing the risks are greater than in other forms of communication because the stakes are higher. At stake are life, salvation, hope, faith, and peace. Is it any wonder that we find it more agreeable to guard our beliefs as closely as we guard our other secrets, including the secret me, and to tend our own gardens?

Much of contemporary religious (notice, I do not say "Christian") thought actually sanctions this quiet, self-indulgent form of religion. Introverted religion preaches the gospel of getting one's head together with the help of Jesus. It is a peculiar blend of pop psychology and spirituality that produces advice like that in the following chapter titles from a typical self-help book on religion:

> How to Overcome Melancholy in Fourteen Days
> Twenty-seven Words to Banish Worry
> How the Housewife Can Avoid Worry and
> Keep Looking Young
> How to Turn Yourself into a Shouting Optimist in One Hour

Luther once described the condition of sinful humanity as "curved in upon itself." His picturesque image of God's would-be butterflies living in cocoons of self-centeredness certainly applies to contemporary religiosity and even to churches so self-preoccupied that they have lost the commitment needed for communication of the gospel.

We do not "get over" the resistance to communication, but God breaks it down. Luther was reflecting on his own experience when he wrote, "When God begins to justify a person, he first condemns him; when he wants to build up, he first tears down; whom he wants to heal, he first batters to pieces; whom he wants to bring to life, he first kills."[2] John Bunyan described this contention with God in his classic autobiography, *Grace Abounding to the Chief of Sinners.* There he confesses to the all but irresistible urge that would come upon him to shout blasphemies during the act of preaching God's Word.[3] We have the Scripture's word for it that when God does make his breakthrough, the man or woman of faith experiences another kind of pain. This is the sense of urgency or frustration one feels when the message is bottled up, when all avenues for communication seem to be closing. Jeremiah confessed,

> If I say, "I will not mention him,
>   or speak any more in his name,"
> there is in my heart as it were a
>   burning fire
>   shut up in my bones,
> and I am weary with holding it in,
>   and I cannot. (Jer. 20:9)

Paul said it more simply: "Woe to me if I do not preach the gospel!" (1 Cor. 9:16).

INARTICULATENESS

But what if you are not good with words? May we be excused from witnessing on the grounds of inarticulateness? The Bible does not gloss over the pain associated with speaking God's Word. The greater the prophet, the greater were the feelings of unworthiness, unreadiness, or unwillingness to speak in the name of the Lord. Elijah cited his record of unappreciated heroics on behalf of the Lord and asked to take an early retirement (1 Kings 19:10). Jonah booked passage on a ship heading in the opposite direction from Nineveh. Isaiah feared that his and his people's uncleanness disqualified him as a prophet (Isa. 6:5). Jeremiah said, "Behold, I do not know how to speak, for I am only a youth" (Jer. 1:6). And Moses, the man who later became God's spokesman in the court of Pharaoh, claimed a speech impediment (Exod. 4:10). The fact that God chose as his chief representative a person "slow of speech and of tongue" surely says a great deal about the power of God that attends his Word! In each instance the Lord did not try to talk the appointee into the job by shoring up his confidence in his own communication abilities. Instead, God reaffirmed his own identity and promised his continuing presence. In most cases God's response carried a promise of intimacy that was hard to refuse. To Moses, God said, "I will be with your mouth" and to Jeremiah, "Before I formed you in the womb I knew you, and before you were born I consecrated you. . . . Behold, I have put my words in your mouth."

In the New Testament Jesus speaks words of extraordinary comfort to the inarticulate:

> "Behold, I send you out as sheep in the midst of wolves; so be wise as serpents and innocent as doves. Beware of men; for they will deliver you up to councils, and flog you in their synagogues, and you will be dragged before governors and kings for my sake, to bear testimony before them and the Gentiles. When they deliver you up, do not be anxious how you are to speak or what you are to say; for what you are to say will be given to you in that hour; for it is not you who speak, but the Spirit of your Father speaking through you." (Matt. 10:16–20)

This may not sound comforting, but it is. Stephen Verney writes: "This is most encouraging, because we generally imagine that evangelists go out as wolves among lambs, strong men, well equipped to answer every question and to rend in pieces every adversary. Knowing that we are not such supermen, we suppose 'evangelism is not for me.' "4 Into a society in which the specialist holds the advantage, Jesus continues to send ordinary people. Into a society in which the slickness of the medium overrides the truth or falsity of the message, Jesus sends us as lambs. These words do more than comfort; they exhilarate and liberate us from the shrewd methods and self-indulgent goals of our own society. With the Lord we pray, "I thank thee, Father, Lord of heaven and earth, that thou has hidden these things from the wise and understanding and revealed them to babes" (Matt. 11:25).

The problem of inarticulateness may be the result of an unas-similated faith, a faith to which the intellect has said yes, but the heart has said no or maybe. It is therefore a faith that has not yet learned to speak. When we learn a new word, it first becomes a part of our passive vocabulary. When we hear it or see it in print, we understand its meaning. The word only becomes a part of us, however, when it moves from the passive to the active vocabu-lary and we claim it as an expression of our knowledge. Simon Peter had taken in a full measure of Jesus' ministry and had some idea of the meaning of the word "Christ." What makes the event at Caesarea Philippi the hinge of the Gospels is that there, in re-sponse to Jesus' challenge, Peter's information reached such a de-gree of assimilation that what had been known to him passively boiled over into active expression. He said, "You are the Christ, the Son of the living God" (Matt. 16:16). However, one does not wait for the magic moment of saturation before speaking, but dis-covers it *in* the act of speaking in Jesus' name. Thus there is some wisdom in the old advice to preachers, "Preach faith until *you* have it."[5]

FEAR

Do you remember the first time you spoke a word of Christ to a nonbeliever? What did you feel? If you are like most Christians, when it dawned on you that you were in a witnessing situation, you felt a knot forming in your stomach as you desperately tried to remember clever arguments for the existence of God. You may have wished for a script (What does the manual say?) or at least a Bible passage! You felt the anxiety of one whose philosophy of life is on the line. You had guessed that moments of ripeness such as this would arise, but you never dreamed that you would feel so forsaken and inarticulate and, as a result, so disappointed with yourself. Instead of witnessing you may have changed the subject entirely ("Who do you like in the Superbowl this year?") or di-verted the discussion from God to religion ("My mother was a Baptist too"). Or with your back against the wall, you may have become defensive or argumentative ("And just how can a person who hasn't been inside a church in ten years criticize modern preaching?") and failed to reflect the love of Christ.

The classic sentence with which Reuel Howe begins *The Miracle of Dialogue* gives definition to our fear of speaking. Howe writes, "Every man is a potential adversary, even those whom we love."[6] We shall not label this universal human instinct "hate," for it is fear more than hate that drives Christians to retreat from witnessing. It is not only the tongue-tied, heart-pounding nervousness we considered in the previous paragraph, but the more deeply rooted dread of the Other, God, which produces guilt, feelings of inadequacy, and spiritual paralysis. And it is dread of the other person, this potential adversary, which is manifested in self-centeredness, hostility, and the inability to communicate. So ambivalence, inarticulateness, and fear remain, these three, but the greatest of these, in terms of its devastating effects in the spiritual life of the Christian witness, is fear.

To the nervous, Christ says, as he does three times in the commissioning of his disciples, "Don't be afraid" (Matthew 10). To the inarticulate he promises the gift of divine speech. To the fearful he says, "There is no fear in love, but perfect love casts out fear" (1 John 4:18).

Once we have met this enemy who lives quite undisturbed in the hollow of the most pious, intelligent, and forward-looking Christians, the other, external obstacles to evangelism recede in importance. Misperceptions, cultural biases, and sociopolitical movements blur the clarity of the Great Commission and create reasons, even excuses, for retreating from the obligation to speak of Jesus. In the following sections we shall look at five such distortions of the Christian witness: (1) incognito evangelism, (2) clerical evangelism, (3) indiscriminate evangelism, (4) electronic evangelism, and (5) political evangelism.

INCOGNITO EVANGELISM

Gabriel Fackre coined the term *incognito evangelism* to describe what can only be called a retreat from the traditional task of making disciples.[7] During the 1960s and early 1970s, Christians joined with concerned citizens throughout America to combat war, racism, and other social and political evils. The issue-oriented approach pursued the betterment of society along pragmatic lines and jettisoned a good deal of the church's vocabulary in the process. Explicit references to God or any theological mandate for action only brought divisiveness to the common cause. Besides, the old sacred language, which for too long had decorated those values and institutions now under attack, had become defunct. We no longer trusted words. The preacher, said Amos Wilder, had become like someone speaking into a dead microphone, and evangelism was reinterpreted to mean the implicit presence of Christians in a secular world.[8]

The struggle against injustice must go on, and the church ought to be present in the vanguard, not in its usual position. But to exercise this shadowy "presence" at the expense of the explicit Word that accompanies and interprets Christian action blurs the difference between the gospel and purely secular forms of redemption. Although the great mass movements in the United States have grown still, the advocacy of incognito evangelism persists among former "movement people" who, for a variety of reasons, have not yet relearned their appreciation of the Word of God. As we shall see in a later section, right-wing evangelists are teaching the church a painful lesson in what happens to the gospel when the authentic Word is silenced or co-opted by political ideology.

CLERICAL EVANGELISM

Rarely does anyone in the church suggest that no one ought to be doing evangelism; what we describe as a retreat from evangelism a bureaucrat might term "reprioritization of tasks." Or "let the preacher do it; that's what we pay her or him for." Ministers usually put the blame for this abberation on the laity and accuse the laity of shirking its Bible-given assignment. Laypeople, however, are only too familiar with the professional cleric's need to control the ministry and to wrap it in the myth of his or her indispensability.

It is not uncommon to hear pastors speaking of their involvement in the church in terms of "my ministry," as though they had taken out a loan with the Small Business Administration and were now the proprietor of a handsome little business. Perhaps this is where the professional model of ministry has done some damage. Whenever we depict ministry in terms similar to the dentist or lawyer hanging out a shingle, we blur a basic distinction between the professions and the work of ministry. These other professionals perform services *for* people; they do not enable people to perform them for themselves. If they did, as any honest lawyer will confess, it would mean professional suicide. The professional ministry too has that instinct for self-preservation that can sabotage the task of equipping the saints for the work of ministry (Eph. 4:12).

In my tradition, when a pastor accepts a call to another congregation, his or her congregation will probably be without full-time professional ministry for several months. We have an insidious little word that describes that pastorless congregation. We say it is *vacant.* When a house is vacant, there is no life in it; when a lot is vacant, there is no house on it; the implication is, when a church is pastorless, there is no ministry in it. Many church members will tell you that it is during the so-called vacancy that the people of God begin to understand and exercise their God-given responsibilities.

Pastors who move into these so-called vacant congregations, expecting to meet decimated and dispirited groups of Christians waiting to hail them as savior, are in for a surprise. Instead, they find people so pumped up and exhilarated by their first experiences of ministry that the professionals feel unnoticed and even threatened.

It is in the vacancies that the care of souls, traditionally the pastor's domain, becomes the work of the deacons or lay ministers who may carry the bread and wine to the hospitals for the communion of the sick. Worship, to which the members had been spectators, now becomes true liturgy (in Greek, the *people's* work). And evangelism, which had been a matter of pastoral "contacts," becomes the responsibility of a wide network of people. What a commentary on clericalism when people learn ministry

best in the absence of the minister! Imagine what any congregation could be where pastor and people are in partnership and the
key signature of ministry is "equipping the saints."

INDISCRIMINATE EVANGELISM

When most people think of evangelism, they imagine (or remember) an awkward encounter between strangers. Buttonhole evangelism indiscriminately confronts non-Christians and Christians
alike with questions of an intimate nature and an ultimate importance: Are you saved? Do you know Jesus? Will you be ready
when he comes? The person addressed necessarily remains an
unnamed "you," for this style of evangelism, with its telephone
surveys, tracts, bumper stickers, and sidewalk ambushes, does
not bother to learn names or assess the life situation of those it
engages. (The television evangelists' computerized letters—"Dear
Brother B-R-U-C-E"—are spiritually and aesthetically tasteless
but financially lucrative efforts to personalize evangelism and
smooth its rough edges. One preacher collects the computerized
names of his contributors and carts them up to the Mount of Ol-
ives for a moment of prayer on his Holy Week special.)

Our theological instincts tell us that we are responsibile for
more than dumping the Word on unsuspecting strangers and run-
ning to the next house or car. In fact, there are those who believe
that the Christian witness does not truly happen through bumper
stickers, specialized mailings, television specials, or even mass
crusades. The early church maintained a healthy distrust for the
mass meeting not only because such meetings were illegal in pre-
Constantinian Rome, but also because they produced superficial,
temporary conversions.[9] To be saved means to be incorporated
into the community of faith, and too few of today's practitioners
stick around long enough to provide the depth of care and fellowship available in the average congregation.

ELECTRONIC EVANGELISM OR
"LET ORAL DO IT!"

If you believe that indiscriminate evangelism is the authentic
New Testament version of the Christian witness, you will agree

with those who would turn over the evangelistic enterprise to the professional communicators, for electronic religion is buttonhole evangelism to the tenth power. It is the genius of television both to exploit and camouflage the impersonality of our era. It exploits it by sanctioning isolation and loneliness as authentic expressions of the Christian religion, thereby robbing Christianity of its essentially communal nature. Its message is the Big Lie: you need not leave the isolation (and the safety) of your TV room to be an authentic New Testament Christian. Television also camouflages the impersonality of this surrogate church by bringing supercharged personalities into our living rooms and introducing them as personal friends. Don't you feel like you *know* Pat, Oral, Rex, Jerry, Jimmy, and all the others? When Oral says, "Something good is going to happen to you," doesn't he mean *me?* The television personalities offer both the *distance* from community the uncommitted always require and the *intimacy* of a no-strings friendship the lonely always crave.

Depersonalized evangelism also seems to have the numbers in its favor. Speaking of Jesus is reduced to audiences, shares, gross receipts, and finally a market. Rex Humbard preaches to more people on a single Sunday morning than Jesus did in his entire ministry; one Oral Roberts special confronts more unbelievers with the gospel than a whole circuit of pastors does in ten lifetimes of preaching from local pulpits. Yet we are or should be reluctant to put evangelism into the hands of the electronic prophets, and we have theological reasons.

Sharing the Word of God is not like a high-altitude mission of mercy from which we drop morsels of the gospel onto faceless targets. It is more like the work of the Peace Corps, where the worker lives in the village, learns the language, catches the local diseases, and offers herself or himself as a token of the greater gift she or he would communicate. There is enough of the New Testament still alive in most of us to remind us that the individualism of the isolated viewer before the Tube of Plenty, as Erik Barnouw has named it,[10] cannot replace pastoral and congregational relationships, corporate worship, community ministry, and regular participation in Holy Communion. What the hymn writer describes, "We share our mutual woes, our mutual burdens bear, and often for each other flows the sympathizing tear," is a high-risk form of human encounter which is simply not possible in the electronic parachurch.

The first Sunday Laura came back to church after Bill died, at the point in the service when the peace of God is shared through handshakes and embraces throughout the congregation, Anne, Fred, their kids, Pastor Morton, and others grasped Laura's hand and embraced her saying, "God's peace be with you." And it was so—in the church.

Throughout its history, television has been for the most part a medium of escape. Human realities have not fared well in their trip through the looking glass. The grinding tragedies which resist happy endings as well as the extraordinary spiritual experiences of ordinary men and women are filtered out, and the viewer is left with a residue of insulting, secularized banter which is supposed to reflect "real life." Watch the commercial networks long enough and you can only conclude that *God* is dead. Watch the religious networks long enough and it's the *world* that disappears into the mists of trivial and sentimental religiosity. Of the "TV stupor" afflicting many Americans, Alexander Solzhenitsyn proclaimed, in his now-famous jeremiad at Harvard, Americans "have the right not to have their divine souls stuffed with gossip, nonsense, vain talk."

How ironic it is that Christians, for whom the cross is the symbol of supreme reality, are capitulating to the medium of unreality by allowing slick religious programming to camouflage the unpleasant realities of suffering, injustice, individualism, political corruption, and *un*successful Christians. The religious tube of plenty replaces the anguish of the man who cried out, "Lord, I believe; help my unbelief" with the more glamorous concept of "Winning with Jesus." The unspoken message of the high-budget production is clear: "This train is heading for glory—or at least a twenty hundreths' share of the viewers who count in this nation! Get on board!" To Simon Peter's faith we now prefer Roger Staubach's or June Carter Cash's, a faith that has been fully validated by all the accouterments of success and power.[11] We are tripping

The Retreat   31

off on success and power much in the way Simon Magus was
when he tried to buy the Holy Spirit, a move which provoked
Peter to explode, "May you and your money go to hell!" (Acts
8:20 TEV).

POLITICAL EVANGELISM

Time and time again the cross has been emblazoned on a war-
rior's shield, a university's seal, or a political party's emblem to
give an imprimatur to a secular enterprise or to transform a
bloody dispute into a holy crusade. Our decade is witness to the
ease with which the religion of the cross has been co-opted by
special interest groups and made to do their bidding. In a recent
election, the cross even became a code symbol for ultraright political campaigns: VO†E. The most visible and vocal bearers of
the evangel today are the politically right-wing evangelists. Their
theology ranges from conservative to fundamentalist to charis-
matic, but their politics are remarkably similar. They un-
ashamedly equate the kingdom of God with the kingdom of the
past. Their kingdom is a simpler day—when kids were polite,
streets were safe, America was boss, men were men, and ham-
burger was fifty cents a pound. It is the kingdom of America—as
legendary, lost, and irretrievable as Atlantis. The representatives
of this kingdom have assured the public that the religion of Jesus
not only condones but actually mandates a beefed-up military,
the defeat of the Equal Rights Amendment, the implementation
of capital punishment, the scrapping of Salt II, and other assorted
fruits of the Spirit. So intimate is the marriage between politics
and religion that it becomes difficult to distinguish the *used* from
the *user*. Is Christianity being co-opted by politics, or is politics
being corrupted by Christian power? It seems to be a textbook
example of a victimless crime.

This confusion is due in part to the church's irrepressible lust
for power and in part to the political system's lightninglike agility
in responding to shifting power centers in this nation. For example, reading from left to right, the system produces as if by magic
(presto!) not one, not two, but three born-again presidential can-
didates in the 1980 election. Or reading from right to left, the

church insinuates three righteous Christians into what might have been a godless political campaign. The difficulty for authentic evangelism in all of this is that the non-Christian hears political positions instead of the gospel. And if they happen to be positions with which he or she does not agree, it is these issues—busing, sex education, censorship, and many others—which become the stumbling blocks and obstacles to faith.

It is only fair to point out that conservatives are not the only people who mush up religion and politics. Liberals who have crusaded against the draft, for ERA, against nuclear power, for abortion rights, and so on have also wrapped their causes in the mantle of the gospel. And now they cry "Politics!" the loudest at fundamentalist successes. Perhaps one lesson in this is that we really *are* political creatures and any attempt to dissociate our political beliefs from our religious values is hopelessly naive.

If we believe Paul in Philippians where he tells us that he rejoices whenever and however Christ is preached, even in rivalry and partisanship (1:15–18), we too will rejoice whenever we see the gospel thriving and will not hesitate to seek out the common mind of Christ that can alone save Christianity from politicization. Without an appreciation of this common mind the church will further degenerate into a cartel of partisan causes and take its place with the AFL–CIO, NOW, AMA, NRA, NEA, NAACP, and many others in the stable of this nation's special interest groups. But is it not possible for Christians and their churches to bring the gospel to bear on the political processes without having it devoured by them? Since this is a book about evangelism, it must be pointed out that we seek a Christian witness, not a position; we are called to season this world, not to regulate it.

But there is more to our political reticence. Questions of pluralism and disestablishment will not go away. "Congress shall make no law respecting an establishment of religion," the First Amendment declares. For a time religious broadcasting networks paid no taxes on the commercial portion of their programming, which consisted mostly of pulp reruns and old movies. That tax haven has now closed. Yet the religious portion of their programming, which closely shadows the format of the secular shows, including variety spectaculars, talk shows, and even soap operas, produces income in the hundreds of millions of dollars, all of which is tax-exempt. Many mainline churches have also taken advantage of the situation to fatten their investment portfolios at the taxpayer's expense. But electronic evangelism's reluctance to open its financial books (the Christian Broadcasting Network, for instance, refuses full disclosure) makes it impossible for the ordinary contributor to know how much money is being taken in and how it is being spent. That the government, through its friendly tax laws, should indirectly sponsor this enormously profitable form of evangelism raises church–state questions and tarnishes the reputation of evangelism.

I suspect that for most people some degree of political awareness plays a part in the recoil from popular evangelism. Vague notions of personal freedom and the individual's right to privacy cause many to shy away from evangelism as it is most visibly practiced in America today. If the Constitution guarantees freedom *of* religion, does it not also guarantee freedom *from* religion or at least from the tract-wielding zealots who work the crowds after football games or who invariably blunder into our castles at mealtimes? You can turn off the television, but not these evangelists. Fanaticism and insensitivity to the rights of others go hand in hand. It is this intrusive insensitivity that worries us. Must evangelism be like that?

Before we turn to the resources for and principles of Christian communication, it is necessary to remember that the gospel is a message before it is a method; indeed, the method is shaped by the message and must be held accountable to it. But what is the message? Chapter 3 will explore that question.

NOTES

1. Reuel L. Howe, *Partners in Preaching* (New York: Seabury Press, 1976), p. 59.

2. "Explanations of the Disputation Concerning the Value of Indulgences," quoted in Heinrich Bornkamm, *Luther's World of Thought,*

trans. Martin H. Bertram (St. Louis: Concordia Publishing House, 1958), p. 170.

3. John Bunyan, *Grace Abounding to the Chief of Sinners* (London: SCM Press, 1955), pp. 52–53.

4. Stephen Verney, *Fire in Coventry* (Old Tappan, N.J.: Fleming Revell, 1964), p. 73.

5. Albert Outler, *Evangelism in the Wesleyan Spirit* (Nashville: Tidings, 1971), pp. 20–21.

6. Reuel L. Howe, *The Miracle of Dialogue* (New York: Seabury Press, 1963), p. 3.

7. Gabriel Fackre, *Do and Tell: Engagement Evangelism in the '70s* (Grand Rapids: Wm. B. Eerdmans Publishing Co., 1973), p. 56.

8. Amos Wilder, *Early Christian Rhetoric* (Cambridge: Harvard University Press, 1964), p. 2. On the notion of "Christian presence," see the critique in George E. Sweazey, *The Church as Evangelist* (San Francisco: Harper & Row, 1978), pp. 26–36.

9. Michael Green, *Evangelism in the Early Church* (Grand Rapids: Wm. B. Eerdmans Publishing Co., 1970), p. 279.

10. Erik Barnouw, *Tube of Plenty: The Evolution of American Television* (London: Oxford University Press, 1975).

11. This is the *impression* given by the Church Growth Movement's doctrine of "redemption and lift." "[When people become Christians] they desire education, at least for their children. They become liberated from destructive habits. They become more industrious. As a result of influences like these, they prosper, become different people, and move up the social scale (hence the term 'lift'). . . . Objective observations of their homes, clothes, cars, and bank accounts will confirm this." Donald McGavran and George G. Hunter, *Church Growth: Strategies That Work* (Nashville: Abingdon Press, 1980), pp. 105–6.

CHAPTER THREE

The Message: God's Story

And we bring you the good news that what God promised to the
fathers, this he has fulfilled to us their children by raising Jesus.

Acts 13:32–33a

JESUS ONCE MOCKED the so-called evangelism efforts of the Pharisees, who expended incredible amounts of energy to gain one proselyte only to make that person a child of hell twice over (Matt. 23:15). What was wrong with the Pharisees' method? Nothing that a good message (good news) could not have remedied! Before the great physicist Helmholtz could understand the nature of vision, he had to do more than study the human eye. He had to study the properties of light. Similarly, the search for the best method of Christian communication must begin with the message itself.[1]

But what is the message? The gospel is like crystal with its countless facets sparkling and reflecting the brilliance of the light. It seems dangerously simplistic to try to capture the light in a series of spiritual laws or propositions which, though easily memorized, may rob the message of its most luminous and human qualities. How shall we begin?

THE IMPORTANCE OF STORY

Chances are you first heard the message of Christ by means of a story someone told you. It may have been mother at bedtime, father at family devotions, a Sunday school teacher, or a neighborhood friend. Try to remember: who first told you the gospel? How did it come to you? When I was a boy, our family had a

35

book of illustrated Bible stories—a bazaar, really, that brought Abraham, Isaac, Moses, Daniel, and Jesus into our home in a way that television never could. Right there in my bedroom, towers to heaven were erected, ordinary women were turned to salt, staffs became coiling serpents, seas parted, the lame walked, boys and girls were raised from the dead, and the Son of God was crucified for the sins of the world. All I remember of my parents' storytelling technique is that the stories were told with such urgency that I was brought to the pleasant (but sometimes unsettling) conclusion that these stories had to do with *my* life and faith.

In the last couple of decades the importance of story has been rediscovered. Of course, story was always there, but modern preoccupation with science, rationalism, and in general things analytic caused us to overlook it. We found it easier to look at the universe (and God and ourselves) as a series of problems to be broken down into smaller and smaller components than to fashion the many fragments of our own making into a coherent whole. Meanwhile as we went on our way making new technologies, we continued to live as we always had—by means of story.

We understand our own lives as a plot (sometimes a very complicated one!) with a beginning, a middle, and an end. We cast our lives as dramas, hoping that the introduction in Act One will progress to a suitable exposition in Act Two, that the climax midway in Act Three will be exciting, and that the denouement at the conclusion will not be too disappointing. We are strange combinations of predictable plots and surprise endings, of stereotyped characterization and improbable acts of freedom. We are like characters acting in an unfinished play. By the time Act Three approaches, the "I" we thought we understood so thoroughly in Act One seems a stranger to us.

We maintain family traditions by means of story. Children implore their grandparents again and again: "Tell us what it was like in the old country. Tell us how it was when you came to America. Grandmother, tell us again, please, how you first met Grandfather on the streetcar and he got up to give you his seat!" The adopted child repeatedly asks her or his parents to tell the story of the events surrounding the adoption. And no word can be omitted from the formula: "And then, of all the babies, you chose me, right?"

Similarly, a nation maintains its identity by means of the stories it tells itself. True, we are selective in our storytelling. Concord and Lexington, Valley Forge, the Father of our Country, Appomattox, the Roaring Twenties may mask as much as they reveal. But the stories are ours. When I was growing up, the historical "tape" I heard played most regularly was the story of the Great Depression, a story that, if heard often enough, will induce economic caution in the most profligate of children! What are the stories my children will remember, by which their lives will be secretly shaped?

The stories we tell ourselves and others are like the dredging machines used to hollow out a great canal. With every pass they cut deeper into our psyches. With every retelling they reinforce our identities as historical, plotlike creatures, so much so that one philosopher speaks of the narrative shape of our consciousness.[2] "We dream in narrative, daydream in narrative, remember, anticipate, hope, despair, believe, doubt, plan, revise, criticize, construct, gossip, learn, hate, and love by narrative."[3] That is to say, we are meant to take hold of the truth by means of story. Our minds are story-shaped.

The Old and New Testaments portray God's saving initiative as a history whose plot (with its countless subplots) runs like a silver thread through the changing political, social, and religious fortunes of a people named Israel. It tells of a God involved in world history, specifically, with the band of slaves whose adventures carry them from the Egypt of the pharaohs to the Rome of the Caesars. And as the adventure continues, Israel (and now the church) accumulates a history to which it looks for assurance and a future toward which it strains in hope.

Israel and the church are communities of storytellers. Although they both developed law codes and systems of doctrine, these are grounded in sacred story. At Passover, for example, when the youngest child asks, "Why is this night different from all other nights," the father will answer in narrative, as Moses instructed the people:

> "When your son asks you in time to come, 'What is the meaning of
> the testimonies and the statutes and the ordinances which the Lord
> our God has commanded you?' then you shall say to your son, 'We
> were Pharaoh's slaves in Egypt; and the Lord brought us out of
> Egypt with a mighty hand." (Deut. 6:20)

When the church found it necessary to consolidate its doctrine
and to teach it to others, it did so by means of narrative. Thus
Luke writes in his preface:

> Inasmuch as many have undertaken to compile a narrative of the
> things which have been accomplished among us, just as they were
> delivered to us by those who from the beginning were eyewitnesses
> and ministers of the word, it seemed good to me also, having fol-
> lowed all things closely for some time past, to write an orderly ac-
> count for you, most excellent Theophilus, that you may know the
> truth concerning the things of which you have been informed. (Luke
> 1:1–4)

Luke was continuing the Hebraic narrative tradition when he
wrote of a God who became involved in history in order to redeem it. In Christ, God bound himself to the limitations of human
stories and became datable, as any child who has ever been in a
Christmas pageant can attest, from those days "when Quirinius
was governor of Syria" (Luke 2:2). But we have gotten ahead of
the story.

THE STORY

Once upon a time there was a Being who was alone. He lived in
no heaven, for there was no hell; and earth, because it did not yet
exist, was not his footstool. He had no name, for there was no
creature to ask it of him or to call upon him. He was alone.

One day the Being created light and divided it from the darkness; then he created the earth with its steaming waters, and finally land. The Being differentiated the teeming life of the
waters from the creatures that cover the land, and everything he
touched was good and beautiful.

With special care the Being made another creature out of the
red clay of the planet. The new being was both like his Creator
and very unlike him. His name was Adam. Like the rest of the

animals, Adam was both male and female; but he was also both clay (humus) and living personality (human), a wonderful mixture of earth and heaven. How different he was from the animals! Adam could answer his Creator. He could look up at the stars in the firmament and wonder at the glory of the Being who had created all for his enjoyment and use. Although he never used the word, his life was a doxology. The great Being and his new being were in perfect harmony.

The new being accepted his relationship with the Creator as a part of the natural ordering of his universe. Perhaps for this reason Adam was unprepared for the catastrophe that overtook him. In his satisfaction with the world and his own nature, he began to forget the goodness and power of his Creator. He no longer looked at the stars as signals of the glory of the great Creator; nor did he relate to his fellow human beings as creatures of the great Being. Adam loved them or hated them for what they were in themselves and disregarded their divine origin. He still possessed the impulse toward worship that was given to him at creation. But now, as a suicidal person aims the revolver at himself, Adam turned this impulse inward and trained it on his own nature. He either neglected the vaunted ability to speak to his Creator or, worse, dissipated into words, words, words—about himself. When he heard the Being's voice, he either remained sullenly silent or answered with a sneer. Because he had forgotten the divine story and his own part in it, Adam had become a stranger to himself.

Everything in human society reflected this rupture of the divine-human relationship. The life that had been good and beautiful became onerous. Adam worked hard for his bread but never felt satisfied. The females of the race became sick to death of bearing children, raising them, and watching them come to no good end. Brother hated brother, and sisters made fools of their parents. Death sprung up in the land; like a clammy, suffocating mist it covered every plant and living creature, including the race of Adam.

The great Being looked upon the misery of Adam and felt the old stirrings of love. He remembered the nothingness from which he had created the earth and, looking at the human chaos, was moved to recreate the human race. This time he touched a man named Abraham, living in one of the planet's fertile regions near a town called Ur. To Abraham the Being gave these extraordinary promises: that his seed would be as numerous as the stars of the sky; that he would give him a special land to call his own; that in Abraham all the peoples of the earth would find a blessing. The Being then bound himself to Abraham and his descendants forever. Through Abraham's descendants, later known as Israel, the human race would be rescued from its chaos of evil and recreated into the Adam originally intended by the Creator.

But the people of Abraham fell on hard times. They migrated to Egypt and there became enslaved to a power greater than themselves. But the Creator Being heard the cry of his chosen people. On the Plain of Midian he appeared to an Abrahamic refugee named Moses. Out of a thorn bush alive with fire, the voice of the great Being called Moses and appointed him to be his spokesman before the court of Pharaoh. Just as Moses was about to depart from this place of revelation and to undertake his mission, he turned and, almost as an afterthought, asked the Deity a simple question: "What is your name?" The great Being replied, "My name is Yahweh (which means I AM). When you go before Pharaoh and the forces of oppression, tell them I AM has sent you. And to your people, say that I am the God of their fathers— of Abraham, Isaac, and Jacob. From the beginning I AM and I WILL BE for you!"

In the name of I AM and I WILL BE, Moses led the people from captivity. Yahweh himself set the people free in an action that identified Yahweh then and forever with the quest for liberation from bondage. In the Exodus he made freedom a part of his and his redeemed people's identity. At Sinai, Yahweh gave the people a pattern for their life under him, the Ten Words, by which Israel would live as his covenant people. The covenant was prefaced by his formula for remembering: "I AM the Lord your God, who brought you out of the land of Egypt, out of the house of bondage."

All sin begins with a loss of memory. Just as Adam lost his own story and with it his own humanity, so Israel soon forgot the great

I AM and his mighty acts. The people of Israel forgot their own story.

But Yahweh did not forget. Just as he had covenanted with Abraham and Moses, he made a pact with David, promising that the Davidic house would always be the vessel of divine blessings for the people of Israel. Under David and his son Solomon, Israel flourished. But the sins of the people were great. With the memory of its own story fading, Israel's political power also waned, and the nation was plunged into civil war, permanent schism, and finally captivity. As the grandeur of David slipped away, there arose the hope of an ideal Davidic king under whom the elusive glory of Israel would be realized. This ideal king would be the Messiah, the annointed One, who would rule Israel and all peoples.

In the generations that followed, Yahweh continued to raise up prophets to prick Israel's memory, but to no avail. Once again Israel went into captivity, this time at the hands of the Babylonians, and it appeared that Israel and the house of David were about to join the Ammonites, Moabites, Perizzites, Edomites, Amorites, and other tribes on whom the curtain of history had fallen. But through his prophets, notably Isaiah, Yahweh promised deliverance and renewal for the people of Israel. A new and unexpected portrait of Israel's deliverer emerged. Isaiah sketched the poetic contours of a figure he called the Servant of Yahweh. The Servant would not come as a mighty military leader but, by bearing the grief and affliction of Israel, would redeem the people through suffering. The hope of salvation, which had been narrowly conceived in terms of the nation, began to take on universal dimensions. Through the suffering and victory of Israel, Yahweh would reveal himself as the God of all people. At the vertex of two intersecting lines of history lay Israel:

The history of salvation had narrowed from Yahweh's creation of the species of Adam to his selection of the race of Abraham and, finally, to his presence in one faithful Servant. But now salvation, once telescoped into the fortunes of one people, had begun to find a wider field. By some miracle Israel's story would one day become the story of the whole human race.

In the meantime, the land continued to be ruled by foreigners: first the Medes, followed by Alexander's Greeks, then the Syrians, from whom Israel briefly struggled free in the Maccabean War, and finally the Romans, from whom there would be no military escape. Thus the universal significance of Israel in the waning years of the Old Testament era was hardly evident in this tiny Palestinian territory governed by Rome. The "light to the nations" had become the plaything of generals, burned over by the fire and chariot wheels of many invasions and refashioned in the image of gods and cultures unknown to Abraham, Isaac, and Jacob.

Through it all the memory of Yahweh did not die. The story was preserved in temple and synagogue worship and in the austere piety associated with the traditions of the Ten Words. Yet the face of Yahweh remained hidden even from his own people. His first "son," Israel, to whom Yahweh had given of himself so freely, had forsaken much of his inheritance and remembered his own story only fitfully. There was more to the story than Israel had ever realized, and only Yahweh could continue it.

The Creator of the world and the Redeemer of Israel raised up a new being—as universal as Adam, as particularly Jewish as Israel—in whom the fullness of Yahweh was pleased to dwell. In many ways the story of this person, Jesus (which means "Yahweh saves"), seems to continue the story of Adam and Israel. In his identity as Jew, rabbi, prophet, and descendant of David, Jesus appears as the logical outgrowth of God's dealings with people. Indeed, Christians make much of Israel's *expectation* of a messiah, as though the priests, shopkeepers, and shepherds of Jerusalem—the average persons on the street—were waiting for none other than Jesus of Nazareth. But the record does not read that way. It reads as a story with which the author has become dissatisfied, so much so that he interrupts the tale and gives it a new beginning. Many of the settings are the same, but the New Testament makes clear in a variety of ways that the story has begun afresh. Matthew begins his version of the story with the words, "The book of the genesis of Jesus Christ, the son of David, the son of Abraham." John begins his version with a retelling of the creation account in which the Word of God (the eternal Christ) pierces the darkness with life and light. John's account might well be called "Genesis II." The book of Hebrews introduces Jesus as a new message "spoken" by the Father. To paraphrase Hebrews: "In many and various ways God told the sacred story to the people of old, but now, at the end of the age, God has told it through a Son. . . ."

One of Yahweh's principles of storytelling is the principle of preparation. Even in a story that has abruptly begun anew, this principle is observed. The prophet John the Baptist appeared in the wilderness of Judea preaching a message of judgment, offering a baptism of repentance, and prophesying of one "mightier than I" to come. In obedience to his Father's will, Jesus went to John and was baptized by him in the Jordan River. A dove descended and lit upon Jesus, and a voice from heaven said, "This is my beloved Son, with whom I am well pleased." With this public "anointing," Jesus began his public ministry, filled with the Spirit and acknowledged by his Father.

Directly from his baptism, the Spirit led Jesus into a wilderness region in Palestine called the Devastation. There Jesus confronted the adversary, Satan, and was tempted. Just as Adam had confronted the serpent in the garden and had been defeated, Jesus faced Satan in the wilderness and was victorious. Just as Israel had wandered through the wilderness for forty years and there had fallen prey to many temptations, so Jesus remained in the wilderness forty days and overcame each temptation. Just as Israel had forgotten the word of Yahweh, three times Jesus refuted the Tempter with a word of the Lord. Jesus bore the accumulated failures of Israel into the wilderness and, by his steadfast reliance on Yahweh, buried them there. His identity as the Son of God had been tested in the molten crucible of desert warfare from which he emerged tempered and strengthened and approved for ministry.

In the ministry of Jesus the rule of Yahweh was established on earth in a way it had never been established during the Old Testament era. Jesus reflected on that rule and explained it to his disciples by means of stories called parables. The subject matter of these parables was as richly textured as a tapestry, but the stories themselves were all cut from the same cloth: the kingdom of God. The parables either tell what the kingdom is "like" or they arise in the context of Jesus' preaching of the kingdom. They do not teach lessons in morals or describe human character. Their primary focus is Yahweh's rulership of the earth. So the one in whom the divine story found its final expression came into Galilee telling stories.

Jesus also expressed Yahweh's authority in mighty deeds called miracles or signs. He healed the sick, cleansed lepers, and cast out demons from those possessed. Although the story was being enacted in the ministry of Jesus, each of these miraculous episodes contains the whole story in miniature. These episodes are paradigms or encapsulations of the larger story of the good news. For example, one day Jesus cleansed a leper (see Mark 1:40–45), an event that revealed a great deal about Jesus' compassion for the afflicted, his authority over the Mosaic law, his power to heal and renew life, and his willingness to sacrifice his own freedom for the sake of others (see especially v. 45). Throughout his ministry Jesus' teaching and miracles combined in an ongoing commentary on each other. His teaching on the rule of Yahweh is illustrated by the mighty signs of that rule; the mighty deeds are incomprehensible apart from his teaching and preaching of the kingdom.

One day on the way to Caesarea Philippi, Jesus asked his friends to make a decision about discipleship. "Who do you say that I am?" Only one disciple, Peter, answered, "You are the Messiah." Soon thereafter, as if to illustrate Peter's affirmation, Jesus was transfigured in the presence of Peter, James, and John.

Appearing before them were the Old Testament representatives of the Law and the Prophets, Moses and Elijah. This was to confirm Jesus' role as the fulfiller of the Law and the Prophets.

From this point on, Jesus' story takes the shape of a travel narrative. From Caesarea Philippi, Jesus set his face to go to Jerusalem, there to endure indignities at the hands of the religious leaders of Jerusalem, to suffer physical abuse, and finally to be executed as a common criminal. In this travelogue (as presented by the evangelist Luke), shabby villages and one-horse towns, shrieking lepers and tricky theologians, adoring children and curious bystanders all seem to fly by as Jesus steadfastly keeps to the road whose destination is death. He is always on the way with the result that his call to discipleship is not "Stand with me," but "Walk behind me." From the beginning his little band of followers was a pilgrim church, always on the way. The portrait of Jesus that emerges in this part of the story is not that of the miracle worker whose power is easy to admire, but the radical prophet whose way of discipleship is hard to follow.

Finally the journey ended when Jesus mounted an ass and made the last mile over the rocky road that took him through the gate of the capital city. At first the road was a boulevard lined with adoring spectators. But the boulevard soon narrowed to a street that led to the high priest's palace and the praetorium of a petty bureaucrat named Pontius Pilate. From Pilate's praetorium, the road became a labyrinthine passage through the halls of betrayal, false witness, judgment, and torture. His way took him out the back gate of the city, where the passage became a thorn-infested path that only one person could walk.

Before we walk behind him on the Via Dolorosa to the Place of the Skull (which is the intention of this story), we must pause to take measure of the distance between the Plain of Midian and the palace of the high priest. Millennia earlier, Moses had stood before the burning bush and asked the Deity a simple question, "What is your name?" Whether the voice thundered or whispered, no one knows. It replied, "Yahweh"—I AM. Years and years later a beat-up and bleeding Jew stood before one of the

bully lords of this world who asked, "Are you the Christ, the Son
of the Blessed?" And in words that must have reverberated in
heaven itself, Jesus replied, "I AM."

The story of Jesus' last week occupies a disproportionately
large section of the four accounts of his ministry in the New Testament. In the 2,197 pages of Boswell's *Life* of Dr. Johnson, the
protagonist's death is dispensed with in the space of 36 pages. In
the scriptural stories of Jesus, the circumstances of his death com-
prise between fifty and sixty percent of the narrative. Until passion week, the story is clipped and pared to essentials. It moves
almost haphazardly from incident to incident without the kind of
temporal or geographical transitions one would expect in a biography. With the passion week narrative, however, the story goes
into slow motion. Every detail is magnified tenfold, and the account loses its choppy quality. Now we see: it is toward this painful witness to the death of Jesus that the story (with its many self-
contained episodes) has been tending. The size of the passion
accounts, along with their cinematic style and attention to detail,
sends a literary signal to the reader and alerts us all to the significance of this impending death.

When death comes, it comes as the sacrifice of an innocent vic-
tim. The Gospels go to great lengths to proclaim Christ's inno-
cence. Caiaphas implies it; perjured testimony slanders it; Pilate
acknowledges it; the centurion confesses it. "Certainly this man
was innocent!" But he had to die. For messianic pretentions? For
fomenting insurrection? For storming the godhead and seizing deity for himself? The tawdry religious and political tale harbors a
secret theme that will burst like a flowering Judas tree when he
is raised from the dead: he died for the sin of the world.

Of his death we may take brief note. Let us say only that he
showed extraordinary kindness toward those who watched him
die and that he died more quickly than those who know about
these things had expected. During his six hours of dying he expressed the full range of human anguish—at the absence of water
and the absence of God—as the darkness gradually extinguished
him. And one more thing: when he finally breathed out the spirit

that had lived in him since his baptism, he cried out, "It is finished!"

It was not a pretty death. When it finally comes, all who have been drawn into this story experience relief. Bach's lullaby in the *Passion According to St. Matthew* captures the peace and the relief of the end.

> Now rests my Jesus peacefully,
> Good night, my Jesus, good night to Thee!
> From all the trials our sin has cost, He is free,
> Good night, my Jesus, good night to Thee.

Before evening, Jesus' body was removed from the cross. It was claimed by a well-to-do member of the Jewish council named Joseph, who had the body placed in a tomb and the tomb sealed with a great stone. The day after Jesus died was the Sabbath. On that day everyone rested, including the dead Messiah.

At Sunday dawn, a few faithful women brought spices to anoint the corpse. When they approached the tomb, they found that its stone had been rolled away. Entering the tomb, they saw a young man, who announced, "you seek Jesus of Nazareth, who was crucified. He has risen, he is not here. . . . But go, tell his disciples and Peter that he is going before you to Galilee; there you will see him, as he told you" (Mark 16:6–7). Trembling and astonished, the women ran away from the tomb.

Only by light of the resurrection did the small group of Jesus' followers begin to reflect upon his ministry and death. Soon they asked, Who *was* this who was crucified and raised again? They began to see clearly what they could not grasp during Jesus' ministry, namely, that he *is* the fulfillment of the Law and the Prophets, that he *is* the Suffering Servant of whom Isaiah spoke, that he *is* Yahweh's only true Son. Through the lens of the resurrection they could now understand how devastating the death of Jesus might have been not only to their own hopes and dreams, but also to the story of the covenant and the righteousness of Yahweh. In the death of Jesus the story had apparently reached its coda. But just as Yahweh created Adam, Abraham, and Israel out of nothingness, so Yahweh recreated Jesus out of death. Just as Yahweh redeemed his first son from oppression, so Yahwah ransomed this second Son from the ultimate prison.

In the resurrection of Jesus the church was born again. Emerging from Judaism, it burst from the tomb of Jesus and opened its arms to the Gentiles, yearning for a time when "all things" would be subject to Christ. For the Christian church, the diagrammatics of history remain the same, but someone else stands at the vertex.

Jesus

Adam→Israel→the Servant   ✝   the Twelve→the Gentile church→"all things"

In the meantime, as the dimensions of salvation began to open and enlarge, the early community's consuming desire was to make its marriage with the risen Lord, to continue to eat and drink at his table, and to tell the world how the histories of Israel, Jesus, and the church at long last had become one story.

CHARACTERISTICS OF THE MESSAGE
On the basis of this story, what may we say of our message? What are its distinguishing features?

Our message is anchored in the biblical narrative. If it loses its anchorage, it becomes a recitation of *my* trials, *my* breakthroughs, *my* growth, and *my* hopes and dreams. Moreover, without this connection to the story, the cherished concepts of love, peace, joy, hope, and the many others that populate the Christian message become detached from their biblical meanings and gain acceptance as innocuous cultural values. As such, they float tnrough our conversations like cudweed on a gusty day, lighting here and there, but without substance and weight to remain.

The gospel is always grace. The story does not become good news if it is presented only as (1) God's condemnation of sinful behavior (law); (2) a list of regulations (for example, church attendance, tithing, abstinence from alcohol) that must be followed if one is to become a Christian (legalism); or (3) a table of pious and popular virtues, be they yesterday's piety, courtesy, and cleanliness, or today's openness, frankness, and freedom (moralism). Most non-Christians identify Christianity with these hard-to-soft versions of the law. This means that the evangelist will patiently hear out the misconceptions and correct them with the true essence of Christianity, which is the good news of what God has done and continues to do for people.

God's story includes me. In the Passover rite the leader says, "In every generation each one ought to regard himself [or herself] as though he [or she] had personally come out of Egypt. . . ." That is, don't just tell the story, but live it; let it live in you. Similarly, the Christian story is lived out among those who are joined to Christ. Paul writes:

> You have been taught that when we were baptized in Christ Jesus we were baptized in his death; in other words, when we were baptized we went into the tomb with him and joined him in death, so that as Christ was raised from the dead by the Father's glory, we too might live a new life. (Rom. 6:3–4 JB)

All new beings in Christ live this single story. When it comes to telling it, the story does not become good news until it finds a human face. It is merely history or "old business" until it grips a human heart and meets a human need.

The gospel contains an imperative. If not, it purveys cheap grace. Most of the apostolic sermons outlined in the book of Acts conclude with an appeal and an offer: repent from the sin that has blinded you to God, and accept the forgiveness God offers you. Jesus called men and women to be not only believers but disciples. His gospel contains the seeds of its own implementation. "Go and do likewise," "Follow me," "Go and sin no more."

God's story is open-ended. Like those who first heard Jesus' parables, we are sent off stage to live them out for ourselves and others. God's story is always straining toward the future. Yahweh said I AM and I WILL BE. Jesus said, "Lo, I am with you always, to the close of the age." The gospel always leaves the door ajar to hope and new possibilities, even in the face of death and the extinction of all our dreams. This forward tilt of the divine story leads us to magnify God day by day and to live as people of hope.

PLOTS AND PARADIGMS FOR
NEW BEINGS

Because the human story takes on many shapes and surprising twists, the divine story too assumes many forms and complexities of plot. There is no one gospel formula nor a single, easily memorized format for presenting the good news. Only if the evangelist is sensitive to the needs and situation of the other person will he or she tell God's story in such a way that it *fits* or *answers* or *completes* or *begins anew* the hearer's story. The simple episodes that follow reflect New Testament pictures based on the four realities most important to Israel's faith and life: creation, exodus, law, and sacrifice.[4]

New creation. John Stockman came up the hard way at American Steel, from office accountant to executive vice-president. Along the way he acquired a weariness with corporate life, a distrust of other people, especially those just behind him on the ladder, and a cynical sense that devalued everything and everyone he touched. As his colleagues used to say, "John knows where the bodies are buried." At age sixty, John had a mild stroke; one year later, his company let him go. He came to Christ—or Christ came to him—not as compensation for a lost world, but as the God who recreates wasted, run-down people. Paul writes, "We know that the whole creation has been groaning in travail together until now" (Rom. 8:22). Although there are many satisfactions in aging, there is also the burden of growing old in a hyped-up society that idolizes youth, despises old age, and denies death. In Christ, John Stockman not only *feels* like a new man, which is the promise of every sleeping tablet and potion on the counter, but he *is* a new being in a way that defeats the desperateness of the old creation.

The eighth day of creation began on Easter morning when God reversed the old world's terminal course. And the new creation through baptism into Christ that God has begun in people, God also promises to extend to the dead lakes, devastated cities, wasted relationships, and all else our hands have touched.

Liberation–redemption. At the age of eleven, Maria had become accustomed to avoiding her mother's "boy friends," who regularly visited the family's apartment in the city's ghetto. These ominous visitors, along with the monthly welfare check, provided support for a family of seven. From her mother, Maria learned the science of survival; from her mother's clients, her neighborhood friends, and schoolmates, she learned the art of escape through the use of hallucinogens. The gospel of Jesus Christ liberated Maria not only from the bondage of sin, but from a sin-engendering situation. The gospel works in the individual heart through repentance and faith, to be sure, but also holistically through communities of people known as the church. Liberation began for Maria when a community of Christ began to affect her world of poverty, drugs, and prostitution. The church did not abolish these realities but, through its counseling and job-training programs, introduced the presence of Christ into them. Maria's entire family, and therefore Maria herself, was affected. The gospel works as a complex of words that cry out for action and deeds that demand verbal interpretation. These coalesce in the church's ministry, a ministry that proclaims *and* reenacts Christ's struggle with the powers of evil. Israel's Exodus meant not only liberation but also redemption: Yahweh was reclaiming these slaves *for Yahweh.* So also the church's gospel of liberation implies redemption, for in Christ God rescues people from bondage, reclaims them, and empowers them to become agents of redemption. To those who belong to alien powers, the Lord says, "If the Son makes you free, you will be free indeed" (John 8:36).

Justification. When David Morrissey was divorced from his wife, June, David's friends assured him that time would heal his wounds. His friends were almost right. In the intervening fourteen years, David quit hating his former wife and gave up blaming his in-laws. His career took an upward turn, and he found happiness with a new wife and family. All that remained from his first marriage was a small spot of guilt on his heart, as indelible as blood on a beige carpet. David and June had a two-year-old daughter to whom, after the divorce, David had ceased to be a loving and attentive father. Over the years he had renewed contact with his daughter, begged from her and even received her forgiveness for his past indifference. But the spot would not come clean. He alternated between the "I'm OK" bravado that denies guilt and the narcissistic self-pity that wallows in it. He even tried church a few times, where he heard a white-robed official say, "I, by virtue of my office as a called and ordained servant of the Word, announce the grace of God unto all of you and, in the stead and by the command of my Lord Jesus Christ, I forgive you all your sins." But to no avail. David's weight of guilt was lifted by no single pronouncement. Through an ongoing relationship with a Christian friend and with a pastoral counselor, however, he began to see that "justification" (a word foreign to most people) means much more than a comfortable familiarity with one's own guilt and a corresponding security in one's own righteousness. It is *God's* judgment and acceptance that counts. The gospel of justification does away with two contemporary fictions: that God has quit judging sin, and that men and women find peace by learning how to feel good about themselves. Justification draws its power from God who, despite all evidence to the contrary, declares us righteous. This God does by looking at us through Christ-colored eyes. "How is it with you and my Son?" God asks. Only then could David let go of his self-preoccupation and begin to rebuild a relationship based on something other than his own guilt.

Reconciliation. They called themselves "blood brothers." At age twelve, Eddie and Mark did the ritual mingling of blood once popular with adolescents and, from that time forward, considered themselves brothers. They were inseparable. They went to school together, played hooky together, delivered their newspapers together. Every morning on their paper route, they paused at the gate of a great stone house with a wrought-iron porch to admire its grandeur and to wonder at what kind of person could own such a house.

In time, however, the blood brothers grew apart. Eddie's superior intelligence carried him through college and into a successful law practice while Mark drifted through a succession of laboring jobs and watched his life flood with disappointment and disillusionment. What had happened to the blood brothers? They had not seen one another in years. One day Mark stopped in front of the great stone house that he and Eddie had admired as boys. As he peered through the lattice of the gate, he saw the owner walking toward him down the long driveway. In dismay Mark recognized his blood brother. Eddie opened his arms and said, "Brother, think of this as your home. Come in." But Mark turned away and fled.

If the blood brothers are to find reconciliation, it will have to be a reconciliation grounded in something more cohesive than their own blood and more powerful than their intellectual, social, or financial differences. "God was in Christ reconciling the world unto himself," says the apostle Paul. That reconciliation presupposes resistance or, to use the image of Ephesians, a dividing wall that must be broken down. It also presupposes a prior action on the part of God, who put forth Jesus as the means by which alienated people might find God and one another. On their own, even blood brothers may never find a common place to stand and embrace again, for reconciliation is the work of God. Its pattern is cross-shaped: God reaches down to us; we embrace one another.

The above episodes do not exhaust the biblical paradigms by which God creates new beings. Many motifs could have been chosen, but perhaps these will open us to the possibilities of story, God's and our own, as a means of sharing the good news.

NOTES

1. Carl Michalson, *The Hinge of History* (New York: Charles Scribner's Sons, 1959), p. 214.

2. Stephen Crites, "The Narrative Quality of Experience," *Journal of the American Academy of Religion* 39 (1979): 291–311.

3. Barbara Hardy quoted in Fred B. Craddock, *Overhearing the Gospel* (Nashville: Abingdon Press, 1978), p. 139.

4. W. D. Davies, *Invitation to the New Testament* (Garden City, N.Y.: Doubleday-Anchor, 1966), p. 310.

CHAPTER FOUR
The Message Refused:
Disowning the Story

For the time is coming when people will not endure sound teaching, but having itching ears they will accumulate for themselves teachers to suit their own likings, and will turn away from listening to the truth and wander into myths. As for you, always be steady, endure suffering, do the work of an evangelist, fulfil your ministry.

2 Tim. 4:3–5

JUST AS THE CALL to witness is met by our own retreat or ambivalence, so the message we bear to the world is often rejected and marked *Refused.* From what we learned about ourselves in Chapter 2, we know that we are, in fact, "carriers" in the sense of being unwitting transmitters of the unbelief that has infected our society. Nevertheless, in faith and obedience we continue to tell the story; but often the story is disavowed or disowned by those who hear it. "That's not my story," they say, and proceed to give their reasons. In the angry disavowals or the polite rejections, the razor-sharp reasoning or clumsy excuses, we hear echoes of our own unbelief, and we learn a great deal about this secular, frightened world we live in.

Two and a half decades ago, the philosopher Bertrand Russell published a collection of essays entitled *Why I Am Not a Christian.*[1] They contain every conceivable reason for rejecting Jesus Christ and his religion, from the economic to the moral to the psychological. Curiously absent from the book is the story of Russell's own moral development. *Why I Am Not a Christian* is a book of ideas, which fittingly climaxes with a debate between Russell and Jesuit philosopher Frederick Copleston over the existence of God. There are not many Bertrand Russells around, articulating their unbelief with wit and philosophical grace. But the person down the street whose church is "the great outdoors" or the beautician who "deserves" some quiet time at home on Sunday morning or the college student who scoffs at this "glorification of unhealthy needs" are all explaining, in their own ways, "Why I am not a Christian."

Evangelism never falls out of dialogue with those who would reject its message. But the dialogue must not proceed as some lowercase version of a philosophical debate over the existence of God, the divinity of Jesus, or the importance of the church. Given the thought and prayer with which you prepare to make your witness, it will not be difficult to win the intellectual contest. In the act of winning, however, you will quit listening, feeling, and suffering with your neighbor and, having won the argument, will have lost the person.

Some years ago the term *anonymous Christian* came briefly into vogue to describe the secret, submerged belief of all who, though explicitly rejecting Jesus, live lives of mercy, justice, peace, and hope. I believe that respect for the integrity of others begins when we recognize the reality of their unbelief. It is condescending to speak only in terms of "shallow excuses" or, worse, to whitewash the fact of modern unbelief with a coat of "anonymous Christianity." All serious objections to Christianity are anchored in unbelief. What follows are some representative disavowals of the story and some typical variations on a common if sometimes camouflaged theme.

SECULAR SUBSTITUTES

One of the marks of any religion is the totality of its claim upon its adherents. The influence of a religion, any religion, will extend well beyond worship practices to include beliefs, creeds, ethics, and worldviews. Secularism, by its total exclusion of the divine from all realms of life, qualifies as a surrogate religion and, as such, takes its place among the other *isms* in the contemporary pantheon. Contrary to popular opinion, secularism ·was not invented after World War II. It is as old as the Enlightenment, whose philosophers destroyed the rational proofs for the existence of God and introduced (in Kant's words) a new "Religion within the Limits of Reason Alone," which replaced divine laws with human values. In response, eighteenth and nineteenth century orthodox theologians reasserted the "facticity" of Christian truth and turned the Bible into a source of proof texts with which to refute the philosophers' errors. In the melee, God's story—as an event to be shared and reenacted in the lives of his people—was lost.

Enlightenment philosophy also spawned political movements, such as our own American Revolution, that upset the "divinely ordained" rule of kings. The masses took control, or tried to, of their own destiny. The discovery of the secular proceeded at a dizzying pace in the industrialization of labor and the mechanization of life. In the nineteenth century, Darwin introduced a new Adam who was wholly a creature of nature. Marx demystified religious beliefs and showed them to be expressions of socioeconomic exploitation. Freud took the lid off human reason and discovered a cauldron bubbling with irrational needs and desires. Nature, which had once declared the glory of God, now seemed to reveal only the loneliness and self-sufficiency of humankind.

Whatever else secularism may mean today, it appears to be a concerted drive toward "reality," a reality from which all that is not essentially human has been removed. The world is cleared of mystery in a manner similar to the way forested land is stripped raw for an asphalt parking lot. We must face the realities of life in our freshly paved civilization, say the secularists, and bid farewell to the mythicoreligious beliefs that have for so long served only as scenery in the "real world."

On the exterior side of the door of our divinity school, some energy-conscious official has placed a sign, "Keep Door Closed." In pencil, someone else has added, "Reality might get in." But what is this so-called reality that can have no place in a school whose curriculum is Jesus Christ? And why must Christ be automatically classified among the phantasms, as though he could be an alien in a world created *for* him?

Our way of life has prepared us for the ultimate in secular substitution. We live imitatively, dressed in synthetic fabrics, fed on powdered fabricated foods, installed in simulated ranches, chalets, and colonial townhouses. Our legal and moral values have been shaped by traditions not our own. We are derivative people whose culture is so imitative that we do not know what to do when confronted by the real thing. What is true of food and furniture is at a deeper level true of religion. We have grown so tolerant of imitation salvation and messiah look-alikes that an encounter with the living Christ at first shocks and then refreshes. An encounter with Christ is a deliciously cold draft of water in the middle of a hot day. That is the way one Samaritan woman found it when she met a mysterious young rabbi who first asked her for water and then offered to slake her thirst for reality.

Before we examine some of our secular substitutes, let us remember that idolatry is seldom overt. Idolatry does not always replace God, but tries to reach God *through* other things and values. This was Israel's folly at Sinai when it tried to worship God *through* a fertility symbol.[2] Perhaps the most difficult of all the idolatries to identify and overcome is the idolatry of believing.

"I believe . . . in believing." Secularism has widely succeeded in drying up the well, but not in abolishing the thirst. It has denied the object of traditional beliefs, but it has not done away with the mechanism of believing. I can remember a time when, if a person did not derive ultimate meaning from Jesus Christ, he or she was thought to be an unbeliever. Today everyone is a believer in something. We are *into* religious, psychological, and philosophical programs the way a small child gets into a cookie jar—or a dangerous medicine chest.

To our fellow citizens, Paul would say (as he did to the Athenians), "I perceive that in every way you are very religious, for you are engaged in the most comprehensive spiritual quest since the Age of Revival. But you hope to find the answer in the spiritual candy store of TM, est, Rolfing, Arica, Zen, biofeedback, astrology, scientology, and jogging. You shave your heads, read your numerology, wear caftans to the theater, and live in communes, seeking the ultimate in human community, which is but a reflection of the community God established with all who are in Christ Jesus. You meditate, but on whom or what you know not. The more sedate among you worship at the shrine of the American Way of Life: U.S. Steel, Little League, *Guideposts,* fair play, pragmatism, and democracy."

"I believe . . . in the American Way." Using a pair of scissors, Thomas Jefferson literally cut out of the New Testament the more objectionable religious passages, leaving what he called "the most sublime and benevolent code of morals which has ever been offered to man."[3] The values Jefferson admired lay at the foundation of our republic and represent the guiding principles by which many live. Generations after Jefferson, an American president, Dwight Eisenhower, was asked about his religion. He replied, "I believe in the American way of life." When Jefferson's (and Eisenhower's) values are cut loose from their moorings in biblical religion, they take the place of God and become objects of belief. America is a nation of incorrigible "belief-ers." The Supreme Court recognized this and gave religious status to any belief that has come "to occupy a place in the life of its possessor parallel to that filled by the orthodox belief in God." In Old Testament language, the value becomes an idol. Something relative has been absolutized.

There is nothing more difficult for the evangelist than to counter a perfectly good value or ideal that has been taken out of order and absolutized. Needless to say, it is not the Christian's business to demean honesty, fair play, competition, or country. When your neighbor begins to spin out the values that have become absolute for her, it is necessary to make her aware of her own belief *system,* that is, her own religion. The evangelist then testifies to the God who does not oppose these values (if that is indeed true!), but who is the author of them. Augustine said, "Where I have sought the truth, there I have found my God, the truth itself." One does not believe in any *ism* the way one believes in God, for belief in God always entails trust in and surrender to another living Being who is the source of humankind's noblest ideals.

MORAL INDIGNATION

"I lead a good enough life." This argument takes us a step beyond adherence to substitute values to a theological justification
of unbelief. Salvation by grace alone is the fundamental proclamation of the New Testament. I do not know of any painless way
to avoid a confrontation on this point. The very notion of unde-
served merit will always rub human reason the wrong way and
incite great resistance. In the testimony to grace, it is not the
evangelist's responsibility to *prove* his or her neighbor's need of
it. Often the Christian witness makes the mistake of trying to con-
vict a neighbor of sin according to the criteria, say, of the Ten
Commandments, before making an offer of God's grace. The witness runs through the commandments expecting to snag an op-
ponent on a sin, only to find that his or her non-Christian neighbor does *not* swear or use witchcraft, construct graven images,
mistreat parents, steal, murder, hate, commit adultery, or covet
anything that belongs to a neighbor. The unbeliever already
knows that he or she commits no such sins. In fact, such knowledge is the ground of that person's security. But that security is
also the person's sin.

When the evangelist asks a neighbor to measure his or her conduct against the Ten Commandments, church traditions, or the
behavior of "good Christian people," the evangelist is presenting
a moralistic substitute for Christianity and is playing the neighbor's game. The greatest sin, the sin which alone has the power
to separate humanity from God, is unbelief. As Kierkegaard
taught, the opposite of sin is not virtue, but faith. Unbelief is not
a failure to state propositional truths about God in orthodox
terms. It is not improper conduct as outlined in the last nine of
the Ten Commandments. These are all symptoms of the greatest
sin. Unbelief, the greatest sin, is a failure to trust in God's
mercy—a failure that manifests itself in rebellion and defiance of
God. The self-righteousness that exclaims, "I lead a good enough
life" reflects polite hatred of God expressed, of course, in the acceptable category of moral worth.

In the moment of debate, those who give vent to this kind of moral indignation see their whole lives pass before their eyes, and behold, everything they see is very good. This uncritical review of their own story or history is then encapsulated into a current assessment of character: my righteousness is second to none. Since there is something of the Pharisee in each of us gloating, "God, I thank you that I am not like other people," perhaps the best approach to self-righteousness is a sharing of stories and a personal word of confession: "I know this goes against the grain of everything we have come to expect. I am always struggling against this, too, struggling against grace, because instinctively I know that this is not my way. The bad news is that we cannot make ourselves acceptable to God. The good news is that we don't have to" (read Rom. 3:19–25).

"The church is full of hypocrites." With this objection, a self-justifying defense has taken to the offense, and it is the duty of the evangelist, who may be under indictment with the rest of the "hypocrites," not to be offended. Hypocrisy is the perennial charge of the skeptic against the Christian church. One need only think of Marx's outraged accusation against Christians:

> Does not every minute of your practical life give the lie to your theory? Do you consider it wrong to appeal to the courts when you are cheated? But the apostle writes that it is wrong. Do you offer your right cheek when you are struck upon the left, or do you not institute proceedings for assault? Yet the gospel forbids that.[4]

Christians do struggle with the discrepancy between what they confess and what they do. But it was not Karl Marx who first isolated the divergence between theory and practice among Christians. Jesus knew of its existence among the Jewish sects of his day and condemned it.

> Woe to you, scribes and Pharisees, hypocrites! for you are like whitewashed tombs, which outwardly appear beautiful, but within they are full of dead men's bones and all uncleanness. So you also outwardly appear righteous to men, but within you are full of hypocrisy and iniquity. (Matt. 23:27–28)

Of his own followers he said, "Not everyone who says to me,

'Lord, Lord,' shall enter the kingdom of heaven, but he who does the will of my Father who is in heaven" (Matt. 7:21).

The outsider who charges the church with hypocrisy has perhaps just discovered the phenomenon of which Jesus spoke. Outsiders may even believe that Christians conspire to act in ways that deny or contradict their stated beliefs. Like the refusal based on self-righteousness, this one also confuses Christianity with moralism. Given the moralistic presupposition, *of course* Christians must live faultless lives! But the evangelist knows and must convey to the objector that Christians are not self-perfected saints but forgiven sinners who daily struggle, fall, repent, and find forgiveness in a merciful God.

Persons who say, "The church is full of hypocrites," have a peculiarly horizontal view of religion. They measure their own goodness against the behavior of other mortals who happen to be members of the Christian church. The unfailing conclusion is always "I am just as good as they are"—a vanishing comfort when one catches the first glimpse into the essence of the gospel. While it is reasonable to expect Christian lives to reflect Christian faith, the truest standard of behavior is not the minister, deacon, or president of the missionary society, but God. "Be perfect," says Jesus, "as your heavenly Father is perfect"—a vertical norm that renders our lateral judgments trivial and irrelevant. If one must make human beings the measure of religious judgments, it is good to remember what C. S. Lewis somewhere said: that one never compares oneself with another person, but rather asks the question, How does my life story with Christ compare to my story without Christ?

THE USELESSNESS OF WORSHIP

Many non-Christians equate the Christian religion with an hour's formal observance of rites and ceremonies on Sunday morning. One who regularly attends such a gathering is termed a "practicing Christian." Of course, there is more to being a practicing Christian than punctual, weekly devotion. But formal worship is a kind of barometer for measuring an entire life of praise, which is what "practicing Christian" really means.

"I don't have time." For creatures set in time and space, this is certainly one of the most fundamental objections possible. It is like saying, "I've run out of air" or "I have nowhere to exist." Time is not a matter of quantity (since everyone has an equal amount) but of decision. When we say we have no time for something, we mean that something is not important enough. When we say we have no time to worship Christ, we mean that we would rather spend our time in other ways. Of course, no one wants it to sound that way; thus the phrase, "I'll get involved when I have more time."

A University of Wisconsin study found that we devote approximately three years of our lives to doing nothing but waiting—for doctors, dates, airplanes, taxis, the elevator, the mail, and many other things.[5] The Christian evangelist will discover that those to whom he or she addresses the gospel are also waiting. They are waiting for the spouse to attend worship services, waiting for the baby to be born or to get past nursery age, waiting till the family room addition is complete, waiting for busy summer to pass into fall or icy winter to pass into spring. In short, they are waiting for the right time. These are people who, for the purposes of religious conversation, talk about time as something that happens to the person. However, the Christian does not passively submit to time, but receiving it as a gift from the Creator, takes responsibility for shaping it to the glory of God. The Bible offers no philosophical treatise on the nature of time; rather, it treats each moment as an opportunity for decision: "Behold, now is the acceptable time; behold, now is the day of salvation" (2 Cor. 6:2).

"I don't need to go into a church to worship God." It may be instructive for the evangelist to explore the private devotional life of the neighbor who does not attend church. The evangelist will discover just how many people do in fact read the Bible and pray daily but have no apparent need for corporate worship. Many who have "made a decision for Christ" may understand the need for a personal, disciplined system of devotion but have no grasp at all of the corporate joy and responsibility of worship. The prevailing philosophy of individualism has convinced them of the

feasibility and even the desirability of doing the impossible: celebrating *solus* (alone).

While the individualist is raising one set of objections to worship, the pragmatist is raising another. "What does worship accomplish? You learn nothing from it. In your praise you do not even ask for specific necessities. The adoration of God yields no return." Such was the implicit objection of the disciples to the woman who "wasted" expensive ointment on the head of Jesus. Jesus' answer, "she has done a beautiful thing to me" (Matt. 26:10), provides a clue to a wholly other and (to us) foreign approach to life before God. This nonutilitarian accent is captured in the first question and answer in *The Westminster Shorter Catechism*. "What is the chief end of man? Man's chief end is to glorify God, and to enjoy him forever." Before worship is a tool of Christian education, a promoter of psychological health, or a "draw" for church membership, it is worship. When worship is undefiled by formalism, and when it is accompanied by "worship in the world," which is mission, service, and justice, it needs no defense.

In addition to prayer and praise, corporate worship offers a public exposition of God's Word. God's written word functions as a personal summons to all who hear it, but the interpretation of this summons, if not shared in the mutual exchange among brothers and sisters, may lapse into private, subjective misreadings of the Word. Paul never envisioned a Corinthian or a Galatian individual curling up in a corner for a silent reading of one of his letters (much less the viewing of worship on television!). God's Word was originally addressed to the church at worship and continues to find its fullest meaning when interpreted by and among the people of God.

"What you say makes sense," says the objector, giving ground, "but isn't it at least *possible* to be a Christian without attending church?" A variant of this comment is, "Since I got saved, I no longer need the church." My response to the first comment is, "It *is* possible, but not for long." And to the second comment, "When you got saved, you got *into* the church." Both objections overlook the sinful, lazy, self-satisfied, backsliding nature of humankind, to which Scripture and experience bear eloquent testimony. Without the nurture of Word and sacrament and the fellowship of other Christians, growth is impossible. And in spiritual terms, if you are not growing, you are dying.

"It's good for the children." Of course it is. But "it" is also good for adults and all people who are searching for peace with God. The phrase, "It's good for the children," usually implies that the children will be sent but not brought to Sunday worship. It may be spoken by parents who believe that by sending their children to Sunday school they have fulfilled their religious obligations toward their children. In this sense the bus ministry, with the minimal demands it places upon parents, may play into the hands of those who believe that religious faith belongs to the realm of Santa Claus, summer camp, scouting, and other childhood experiences.

The parents who sincerely wish to drill religion into their child will be disappointed when, at an early age, the child notices that his or her parents want no part of Sunday worship and begins to copy their indifference. Church and Sunday school are not substitutes for the shared life of faith in the home. Communication of the Christian faith by parental edict rather than by example does not work.

Parents who send their child to church ought to examine their motives. Perhaps they see Christianity as an ally in their attempt to civilize their child. They may believe that in Sunday school the child will learn to sit still and listen, to socialize with others, or to respect elders. In this misunderstanding of Christian education, Sunday school becomes a finishing school, and the gospel is perceived as a tool in childhood development. This "it" that is good for the children, however, is not an introduction to socially acceptable values, but the good news of God's special friendship for them in Jesus. It is the saving message with which the children in due time may evangelize their parents.

"I was forced to attend as a child." With this excuse the evangelist may be drawn into an involved psychological explanation of

why the neighbor or friend avoids worship and ignores the claims of Christ. Actually, this explanation is no more compelling than "I was forced to brush my teeth as a child." It is the parents' God-given responsibility to rear their children in the Christian faith.

With this objection the evangelist has the opportunity to distinguish between religion as an onerous duty and religion as joy in the gospel. I am constantly perplexed and discouraged by the great numbers of people who view worship attendance as an unpleasant, disciplined confinement. Parents, with their legalistic methods, and churches, with their predictable formality and boring sermons, cannot evade much of the blame for this negative reaction.

At the end of many of our worship services, the minister says to the congregation, "Go in peace. Serve the Lord!" This charge is undoubtedly a carry-over from the priest's dismissal of the people at the end of the mass: *Ite, missa est*. These Latin words can mean, "Go, you are released" or "Go, you are sent." Which shall it be? It's up to the church to foment such celebration of the good news that departing worshipers will never feel as though they are released from another hour's confinement, but sent by God as ambassadors.

INTELLECTUALIZED RELIGION

The evangelist rarely encounters genuine intellectual objections to the Christian faith. In my experience few people have objected to the logical contradictions in the doctrine of the Trinity, the improbability of divine omniscience, or the doubtfulness of prayer. Where objections of the head are raised, they are usually a prelude to deeper questions of the heart. It was Pascal who said, "The heart has its reasons which reason knows nothing of." Therefore, the evangelist should not become so involved in reasoning through the intellectual arguments that he or she forsakes the personal, warm witness to the truth that surpasses human understanding.

"How can a good God allow so much suffering in the world?" Such a question may be an intellectual exercise or a personal ag-

ony. The good listener will quickly distinguish between the two and frame his or her response accordingly. The question of suffering presupposes the mystery of the origin of evil, which twenty centuries of philosophy have failed to explain. The evangelist has no desire to make short work of God's mysteries by converting them into problems. We do not owe our neighbor an explanation. We owe our neighbor a witness.

Nevertheless, though the gospel may not solve the question of suffering, it speaks to those who suffer.

1. Suffering has no place in the original, creative purpose of God. But humankind's separation from God brought with it physical and moral evil, the pervasiveness of which Paul alludes to as the "reign" of sin and death. This is where we are, and it is intellectually and historically impossible to get behind or outside this condition in which sin, suffering, and death envelop us as indissoluble elements of a lethal atmosphere.

2. Because of the universality of this condition, it is not possible to identify the specific causes of suffering. Job asks in effect, "Why me?" "Why hast thou made me thy mark?" (Job 7:20). The voice from the whirlwind never gives Job an explanation, but only an affirmation of the reality and majesty of God.

3. God does not speak clearly about suffering, but in the incarnation of Jesus, God speaks a definitive word to those who suffer. The life and death of Christ mirror God's willingness to enter the human experience of suffering; in the crucifixion, God's Son bore the pain of the world; and in the resurrection, God entered the lists against the finality of death.

In one of the most haunting passages in Western literature, Elie Wiesel, himself a survivor of the Holocaust, writes of the presence and absence of God at Auschwitz. He tells how one day the SS hanged a boy in front of the whole camp. Wiesel remembers what he heard: " 'Where is God? Where is he,' someone asked behind me. . . . For more than a half an hour he stayed there, struggling between life and death, dying in a slow agony under our eyes. . . . Behind me, I heard the same man asking: 'Where is God now?' And I heard a voice within me answer him: 'Where is he? Here he is—he is hanging here on this gallows. . . .' "[6]

4. The same God who made the world and everything in it does not abolish pain and suffering, but to those who are in Christ, God promises divine presence, peace, and strength.

5. God's ultimate purpose, as expressed in the creation of a whole and good world, will not be forever thwarted. At the end of the age when Christ becomes "all in all," suffering will end and its redemptive nature will be revealed. We see this redemption-in-suffering now darkly, as through a glass.

> We are afflicted in every way, but not crushed; perplexed, but not driven to despair; persecuted, but not forsaken; struck down, but not destroyed; always carrying in the body the death of Jesus. . . . (2 Cor. 4:8–10)

To the parents whose child has died, to the invalid whose only visitors are the physical therapist and the pastor, to the bitter wife whose husband has deserted her, in short, to all who suffer, the evangelist brings a ministry of compassion. The person who mourns with Job, "I will complain in the bitterness of my soul," desperately needs a helper. The argument concerning suffering requires a relational before a rational answer. It calls for Christian love, understanding, and prayer. For now, that *is* the answer.

"Any religion is OK. We're all heading in the same direction." The key to this objection is indifference. Your neighbor does not really want to debate the tenets of Taoism over against those of Christianity any more than he or she wishes to stand up for Presbyterianism as opposed to Methodism. If any religion is OK, then none can make a claim on the person. A variant of this approach is a religion of sincerity: "I don't care what a person believes, as long as the person is sincere!" This relativistic approach overlooks for the moment the fact that some of history's most misguided "saviors" have been the most sincere.

Studies in anthropology and the history of religions have unearthed a fantastic network of formal similarities among the great religions of the world. Psychologists of religion point to the shared subjective or mystical experiences of all believers, whether believers in Jesus, Buddha, or Mohammed. Comparative religion reminds us of the nobility of Buddhism, the versatility of Hinduism, the resiliency of Judaism, the wisdom of Confucianism, and the creativity of Christianity to the end that Christianity's claim to exclusiveness, based on the absolute claim of Christ, seems parochial and unreasonable.

"I am the way, and the truth, and the life; no one comes to the Father, but by me" (John 14:6). "And there is salvation in no one else, for there is no other name under heaven given among men by which we must be saved" (Acts 4:12). God's words are never scattershot into the air but are always addressed to someone, in this case, to *us*. If we rationalize God's words away, we cease to be hearers of these words, for we have removed ourselves from their audience. No one who has been seized by the goodness of God and has heard the call to discipleship will look for other ways or stumble on the stone of relativism.

CHURCH: WARTS AND ALL

"The trouble with the church is. . . ." This sentence has as many endings as there are institutions and congregations that identify themselves as "church." The existence of imperfections in the church is not an insignificant argument against the Christian faith. After all, the church is the instrument chosen by God to effect God's presence on earth. If after 2,000 years the church still lags behind the message of its Founder, that failure may say something about the viability of the message itself. If the church is not able to live or live up to its own story, perhaps there is something wrong with the story. This is the sober side of any examination of the trouble with the church.

Usually, however, various criticisms of the church point to specific denominations or congregations. "That congregation is too high-church." "That church cares only about my money." "When the church ordained a homosexual, that was the last straw." "That church does nothing for the community but give chili suppers." "There's nothing wrong with that church that a good preacher wouldn't cure." "Church politics turns me off!"

When someone begins a sentence with the phrase, "The trouble with the church is . . .," we must listen carefully to discover if the outsider has caught a glimpse of something we are unable to see. We who are so quick to unmask the idolatries of our culture may have little insight into the many ways we have made an idol of "our church." We who are too ready to criticize those who leave the church may not have sensed the hurt and frustration of those who feel the church has deserted them. So preoccupied are we with the mechanics of the church that we often fail to address or even to see the world's contempt for it.

The test of the church is the living presence of Christ in it. The paradox of the church is that in its disunity and weakness it retains its identity as the body of Christ. When the real presence of Christ among his people is forgotten, the church forfeits its identity and becomes a society for the preservation of doctrine, polity, or liturgy. It gradually begins to lose the properties of a healthy body—warmth, vigor, flexibility, growth, and susceptibility to pain; it remains a body but in another, deadly sense.

Before we stoutly defend the peculiarities of the church, we would do well to acknowledge its sins and imperfections and to give thanks to God for accomplishing the divine purpose through these imperfect vehicles and in spite of them. In an article entitled "A Layman Looks at His Parish," Clifford Morehouse writes:

> How does my parish look to me, a churchman? It is a poor, worldly thing, often concerned with petty matters. Yet it is the doorway to the Great Church. It is often hopelessly behind the times; yet it is the gateway to the future. It is often torn by controversy; yet it holds the key to eternal harmony. . . . It seems to have little influence on the community; yet without it the community would be a poor place to live in. Its budget it small, and hard to balance; yet within it is to be found the great treasure. Its missionary flame burns low; yet through it men are sent forth to preach the Gospel to all nations. It is full of sinners like me; yet it is the mother of saints. In the eyes of the world it is a poor and perhaps a pitiful thing, one that can be easily overlooked or ignored. But in the eyes of God it is His Holy Church, the manifestation of His presence in that particular corner of His world. My parish may seem weak, inefficient, inadequate and worldly; yet it is my link with the Great Reality. It is the very means by which God comes down to earth and dwells among His people.[7]

This chapter set out to be a survey of the many ways in which God's story is disowned by those to whom it is told. But little has been said about story, and that is the key to understanding those who reject the Christian message. Most of the objections operate on an intellectual level. They may have been triggered by life-story experiences, but those who express them have not made the honest connection between their own stories and the beliefs they are rejecting. By intellectualizing their objections to the gospel, they are dismissing the power and the "livability" of the Christian story. They have imprisoned the story in the mind and barred it from life.

It seems to me that the most freeing approach is the one that enables the non-Christian to tell his or her story as completely as possible. That means that instead of debating ideas, the evangelist will listen carefully for the narrative elements of all objections, the stories of "When I Stopped Believing" or "How I Quit the Church," and relate these both to the evangelist's own story and to one of the subplots of God's story. The purpose of this method is not to rubberstamp or affirm the unbeliever's misperceptions; nor is it merely to allow the objector to release pent-up feelings of anger toward God or the church, although this may be important. Our ultimate purpose is to help the non-Christian understand that his or her story need not be finished (as a stage of development or chapter in one's life), but that even the story of one who has rejected God can, by the grace of God, begin again.

NOTES

1. Bertrand Russell, *Why I Am Not a Christian* (London: Allen and Unwin, 1957).

2. D. T. Niles, *The Message and Its Messengers* (Nashville: Abingdon Press, 1966), pp. 62–64.

3. *The Adams-Jefferson Letters,* vol. 2, ed. Lester J. Cappon (Chapel Hill: University of North Carolina Press, 1959), p. 384.

4. Karl Marx and Friedrich Engels, "The Leading Article of No. 179 of *Kölnische Zeitung*" (1842), *On Religion,* trans. not noted (New York: Schocken Books, 1964), p. 35.

5. Charles A. Reimnitz, "What Time Is It?" *The Cresset* (November/December 1977), p. 43.

6. Elie Wiesel, *Night*, trans. Stella Rodway (New York: Hill and Wang, 1960), pp. 70–71.

7. Quoted in George Hoyer and Justus Kretzmann, *In Time . . . for Eternity* (St. Louis: Concordia Publishing House, 1963), pp. 184–185.

CHAPTER FIVE

Resources for Christian Communicators

For I am not ashamed of the gospel: it is the power of God for salvation to every one who has faith. . . .

Rom. 1:16

THE MOST PROFOUND yet most unnecessary burden any evangelist bears is loneliness, not merely isolation from the company of Christians within the circle, but a deeper estrangement from all the comforts of God. This sense of going it alone is doubtless heightened by our secularized society in which, as Bonhoeffer prophesied in 1944, even Christians live as though there were no God, yet always in the presence of God![1] Godlessness is ultimately repressive, for it relentlessly drives us back upon our own resources, the bankruptcy of which only confirms the futility of speaking of Jesus in our generation. God commands us to speak in a seemingly impossible situation of unbelief. Is that fair? Would God commission us to speak without adequate resources, the way a desperate general might dispatch untrained adolescents to the front line? The writer of Ephesians commands Christian soldiers to "put on the whole armor of God," that is, the breastplate of righteousness, the shield of faith, the helmet of salvation, and the sword of the Spirit (Eph. 6:10–20), all summed up in the phrase "the equipment of the gospel," to which we now turn as a resource for communicating Christ.

BAPTISMAL IDENTITY

Witnessing begins with identity. It is not enough to master the *what* of the message and the *how* of the method without the *who*

of the messenger. The lawyer's first directive to the witness is
"State your full name." Who are you? How are you involved in
this case?

For the Christian witness, the question of identity is more complex. William Sloane Coffin is fond of challenging his young audiences with the question, "Who tells you who you are?" Other
questions are, What parent? What institution? What B+ captures your effervescence? What professional accolade completes
you as a person? At the office or factory, in the complex web of
social and family relationships, who tells you who you are? These
questions recognize the derivative nature of all identity; in no
sphere of life is there such a creature as a "self-made person."
And nowhere do young men and women cry out "I am somebody" unmindful of the shadowy suspicion that stalks us all: "I
am nobody."

Who are you? State your full name. The child is born a cipher;
on its birth certificate it will be assigned a number, the first of
many. Later will come draft and social security cards and ID
numbers of all sorts. As the child grows to maturity, he or she will
complain, as most of us living in the second half of the twentieth
century do, about being a number or a cog in a machine.

In baptism we received an identity—not a number and not just
a name to be misspelled, computerized, and finally buried with
all the other names. But in baptism we become somebody in
God's church, and our name was then and is now inextricably
linked to another name and to another identity. We became
somebody in the name of the Father and of the Son and of the
Holy Spirit. In baptism we were sacramentally joined to a history
or a story. The story of Christ's death and resurrection was reenacted in us when we were buried with him beneath the waters
of baptism and raised with him to newness of life (Rom. 6:1–4).

When the times of spiritual drought come upon us, when we
would cry out with the poet Hopkins, "Mine, O thou lord of life,
send my roots rain," the renewal we seek is but a remembering.
Much has been written recently about spiritual rejuvenation and
"How to Be Born Again," as though we might engineer our own
spiritual health the way we shape our tummies or color our hair.
Baptism sets us free from the self-help heresy and reminds us

that, just as God covenanted with Israel, so God once made a covenant with us in the water and the Word and will not break it.

The boy stands as a child before his father for the last time. Early in the morning he will leave for boot camp. There isn't time to say all that needs to be said, so the father must be content to say, "Remember who you are." There is no aristocratic family name to be upheld, no exalted reputation to save. Could this be the father's way of saying, "Remember your baptism?" When you go to work or school or war—or to witness—remember who you are.

THE LONG LINE OF WITNESSES

What Bernard of Chartres wrote long ago might be said of contemporary Christian witnesses: "We are like pigmies standing on the shoulders of giants. We see further than they but only because we are standing on their shoulders." The rhetoric of some church and parachurch organizations leaves the impression that evangelism was invented in the second half of the twentieth century or that the Holy Spirit has somehow taken a great leap from the primitive church to the present age without lighting on any intervening era. The Christian communicator needs a sense of history to understand that a linear relationship exists with Christian witnesses of all ages, stretching as far back as the apostles, but not excluding Ulfilas, the apostle to the Visigoths; Patrick, missionary to Ireland; Boniface, sent to the Germanic peoples; Francis of Assisi; Francis Xavier of India; August Hermann Francke and the Danish-Halle mission; Count Zinzendorf; the Wesleys in America and England; William Carey, who founded the Baptist Missionary Society; Walter Rauschenbusch, who ministered to "Hell's Kitchen" in New York City; Mother Teresa of Calcutta; and a galaxy of others upon whose shoulders we gratefully stand.

A noble army, girls and boys,
With men and women saved,
Around the Savior's throne rejoice,
In robes of light arrayed.
They climbed the steep ascent of heav'n
Through peril, toil, and pain.

O God, to us may grace be giv'n
To follow in their train![2]

But the twentieth-century church should also know that it is not called to recreate the primitive church. Just as God created it to be the church of its day, God continues to gather a people in every era. To attempt to recreate the social, economic, and even ecclesiastical conditions of the early church and to impose them on today's church would obscure our mission to the people of our day. We would find ourselves retreating from problems spawned by technology, global scarcity, nuclear war, and a wide variety of peculiarly twentieth-century problems. Our evangelism takes its life from the living Christ proclaimed by our spiritual fathers and mothers, but its field and methods are as current as today's needs.

Our relationship to the rest of the church is also familial. In baptism God signs our adoption papers and welcomes us into the family. The early church understood baptism as each person's "ordination" to a life of ministry among the brothers and sisters, and of witnessing in the world. What brothers and sisters do best is pray for one another. Therefore, it is essential that the members of the church support and pray for those who have ventured outside the security of the family circle to dialogue with non-Christians.

In his engrossing book, *Amen: The Diary of Rabbi Martin Siegel*,[3] the author, a Reformed rabbi on Long Island, addresses the question of family when he seeks an answer to the question: What does it mean to be a Jew? Is Jewishness based on blood, nation, a belief system, or a way of life? When Rabbi Siegel writes, "I don't believe in God, but that has nothing to do with being Jewish," that is his provocative way of de-emphasizing the importance of belief in favor of a way of life. To be Jewish, he says, is to experience the traditions, morality, heritage, and identity which is Judaism. It is to *belong*.

Because Christians are so much more diverse in complexion, lacking the Jewish emphasis on family, tradition, and the whole memory of suffering, Christians tend to identify themselves by their belief systems. In a typical suburban parish, for instance, the families are drawn from thirty separate communities or developments scattered throughout a huge megapolitan area. They have no common ancestral home or cultural heritage (other than the civilized West); their children attend different schools; they shop in different consumer centers euphemistically designated "plazas"; they never meet strolling down some bygone, tree-lined Main Street. At best, they occasionally catch a glimpse of one another across the median of a six-lane highway glutted with cars twenty-four hours a day and euphemistically (again) known as a "boulevard." Their way of life is an American commonplace.

In this church, as in the churches serving communities like this one, the members rush into the building with their personal beliefs learned in Sunday school and catechetical classes, and then rush out, going their separate ways. Where Rabbi Siegel advocates community for its own sake and ignores belief, many Christians concentrate exclusively on keeping their belief systems intact while ignoring the common life in the community of faith. The American woods are filled with so-called Christians who can give all the right answers from the Bible or catechism, but who are novices in the experience of Christian community.

What this combination of individualistic theology and impersonal life style does to Christian communication is disastrous. To many Protestants evangelism means changing or trying to change another person's system of beliefs, usually within the span of forty-five minutes. But evangelism may begin with honest and personal witness that culminates in nothing more than an invitation to the experience of God's family. "Be with us; let's be in the Word of God together over a period of time. Try our family."

THE KEY TO THE SCRIPTURES

Before speaking of Jesus, one must encounter him in the Bible. The evangelist reads God's word devotionally and meditatively. This paragraph takes into account the special sin of the so-called student of the Bible, whether clergy or lay, which is searching the Scripture for information, ammunition, data, facts, or course preparation. There is nothing inherently good about reading the Bible unless one is searching for God in it. To the Pharisees, who had made a golden calf of the Scriptures, Jesus said, "You study the scriptures diligently, supposing that in having them you have eternal life; yet, although their testimony points to me, you refuse to come to me for that life" (John 5:39–40 NEB). Luther once said that bibliolatry, the veneration of the Bible for its own sake, is like cooing over the cradle rather than the baby in it. The Bible is the cradle of Christ.

Sometimes Christians read the Bible for the wrong reasons. The Bible may be reverenced as an almanac, a country storehouse of all kinds of bits and pieces of information or, occasionally, as a geology or biology textbook containing a scientific report of how the world began. Sometimes its prophetic books are viewed as a mumbo jumbo of sacred utterances, including predictions concerning Adolf Hitler, the Common Market, the cold war, and even cobra helicopters! When the Bible is approached in this spirit, it remains a dark book with no key to unlock its mystery. Each generation will discover in it what it pleases, and each generation will find itself at the mercy of charlatans who elevate themselves above the unenlightened masses and alone claim to possess the combination to the Scriptures.

The evangelist must be as well-versed in the Bible as his or her ancient counterparts were when they witnessed in the synagogues and argued with meticulous detail from the Old Testament Scriptures. They did not apologize for the authority of the Word. But also like the ancient evangelists, the contemporary communicator allows the Bible to speak of whom it will: the Scriptures testify of Jesus. Luke tells us that when Jesus dialogued with the men on the road to Emmaus, "he interpreted to them in all the scriptures the things concerning himself" (Luke 24:27). The Word does not necessarily work through simple recitation or cannon-like bombardment, but through *interpretation*. And Jesus is the key to the interpretation of the Bible. As when all the witnesses at his trial pointed to him and said, "That's the one," so every word of the New Testament cries out with Pontius Pilate, "Behold the man!"

The Bible is not an ordinary history book but, as Fred Craddock says so ably of the Gospel of Luke, it tells what *really* happened, giving us the divine perspective on history that transcends the mere recitation of human occurrences and achievements.[4]

This is obviously true of the Gospels, which are not merely cor-
related biographies of the greatest religious genius who ever
lived. Can we imagine a modern biography, say of John F. Ken-
nedy, that would not include a description of his appearance? Or
in an era that has discovered the importance of early childhood
formations, is it possible to imagine a biography that would omit
references to childhood and parental influences as well as to rec-
ords of the adolescent years, schooling, formative teachers, voca-
tional decisions, feelings about sexuality, and indeed the whole
development of personality? The four Gospels omit all this and
more! John the evangelist admits the omissions, "Now Jesus did
many other signs in the presence of the disciples, which are not
written in this book," and states the purpose of his Gospel and the
entire New Testament: "but these are written that you may believe that Jesus is the Christ, the Son of God, and that believing
you may have life in his name" (John 20:30–31).

The Bible is an address, a summons, an invitation which, alone
of all the works of antiquity, travels the centuries and claims us.
If we are to bring the good news to others, we must first let this
book evangelize us. We will ask critical questions of the Scripture, indeed the most critical questions possible. How is God
speaking to me and my community in this word? What human
failure or sin does this word expose in me and my church? Does
this word pulverize me (as Luther said the Word of God can do)
or does it heal me and make me whole? How has this biblical
story been reenacted in my own life or in the life of someone I
know? To what aspect of my lost condition does this word speak
of hope? From what bondage does it liberate me; from what sin
does it cleanse me; over what weakness does it empower me?

It will not do to read the Bible as a collection of proof texts for
evangelizing. First, one must encounter Christ in the Word, be
claimed by him, and be opened to the power and possibilities of
his resurrection. Then there will be time and courage enough for
witnessing.

I once witnessed a debate between a young Christian theology
student and a Marxist professor on the subject of salvation. The
Marxist was forever thumbing through his New Testament (in

Greek) to make this or that point, each one prefaced with an
"Aha!," when he noticed that the Christian was not consulting his
Bible and in fact did not even have one. Genuinely offended, he
asked, "Where is your Bible?" The Christian replied, "In here,"
and pointed to his heart. The young man had done what an effective evangelist must do. He had internalized the Word of God; he
had made it a part of him. He had achieved fidelity not only to
an extrinsic word, but had grown to love what God commands
and promises. God's Word has that capacity to transcend printed
letters on a page and to take shape in the lives and stories of
God's witnesses. This is what Paul meant when he wrote to his
friends in Corinth,

> You yourselves are our letter of recommendation, written on your
> hearts, to be known and read by all men; and you show that you are
> a letter from Christ delivered by us, written not with ink but with
> the Spirit of the living God, not on tablets of stone but on tablets of
> human hearts. (2 Cor. 3:2–3)

THE WORD THAT WORKS

If someone says "word," most persons "see" the image of a typed
or printed symbol. Our cultural perception has so long been dom-
inated by the visual—script, print, electronic image—that we
need to be reminded that the words we see are also symbols of a
more fundamental reality, namely, words as sound. Words are for
speaking and hearing.[5]

Although the sound of the spoken word is the most elusive of
sense objects, it is the most alive and real of all. The spoken word
is clothed in the personality and presence of the speaker. It is
now. It has the capacity to create a bond between communicators
that books, films, and even live television programs may not be
able to duplicate. For confirmation of this difference, compare the
experience of sitting in the fourth row at a performance of a
Shakespearean tragedy with the experience of watching the same
play on television. The word alive has incomparably more power.
Alec McCowen has captivated audiences in Europe and America
with his dramatic presentation of *The Gospel of Mark*. It is the
same old Gospel, word for word, that we have been reading for

years, but in its oral rendering the Gospel has made a new and surprisingly powerful impact on its listeners.

Say "Word of God" and most of us will form an image of a book called the Bible. Before the Word of God was a book, however, it was an oral message. Before it was rendered into written symbols on a page to be devoured by the eye, it was a clarion proclamation or a story or a teaching apprehended with the ear by all to whom the Spirit had given "ears to hear." Before the gospel was a literary masterpiece, it was an invitation to new life in Christ.

Although the Old Testament contains no philosophy of language, it clearly assumes that human speech is derived from divine speech. For the Semite, words do more than symbolize or refer to other realities. The spoken word calls new realities into existence and creates new possibilities for those on whom the word falls. Out of the primeval chaos God said, " 'Let there be light,' and there was light." It is death to see this God, but he may be known in his speaking. Unlike the neighboring deities (and unlike Israel's own idols), this God is far from mute.

In the New Testament the word that gets things done is called the gospel or the Word of God. In the book of Acts, where "Word of God" is a technical term for the preached gospel, we read that this message "increased" (6:1), "grew and multiplied" (12:24), and "prevailed mightily" (19:20). But how does one take hold of this God who cannot be seen? And how does one lay claim to the evanescent Word that glitters like a flame but defies capture? Only one way, says the Bible: by faith. And how does faith come to be? Only one way, says Paul: faith comes by hearing. "We conclude that faith is awakened by the message, and the message that awakens it comes through the word of Christ" (Rom. 10:17 NEB).

To tell the story of Christ, then, is to *participate* in the Word of God. It is not accurate merely to list the Word as one of the resources available to Christian communicators, for the Word works *through* evangelists of every generation, including our own. The Word is larger than the sum total of speakers and listeners throughout the world. When one person shares the message of

Christ with another, that constellation of personalities, sounds, silences, Spirit, and response *becomes* in that instant a Word-of-God-event. The ancient power happens again: the Word creates faith, faith finds expression in words, the words of faith create new faith, that faith, in maturity, will also seek to express itself in words. If we try to look behind this process to a time when words were not creating faith, we fail, for we arrive at that Word about whom the author of Hebrews says, "In many and various ways God spoke of old to our fathers by the prophets; but in these last days he has spoken to us by a Son . . ." (Heb. 1:1–2). Nor is it possible to imagine a time when the earthly church will no longer need this faith-engendering process, when faith will come by some other means than hearing the Word of God. The work of evangelism will endure as long as the church endures. And the church will endure only as long as the Word of God continues to work through men and women who transmit it.

The most beautiful expression concerning this Word that works is in Isa. 55:10–11.

> For as the rain and the snow come down from heaven,
> and return not thither but water the earth,
> making it bring forth and sprout,
> giving seed to the sower and bread to the eater,
> so shall my word be that goes forth from my mouth;
> it shall not return to me empty,
> but it shall accomplish that which I purpose,
> and prosper in the thing for which I sent it.

Of course, there will be moments of disappointment and futility, and we will be tempted to test this promise by tracing the effectiveness of the Word in the lives of those to whom we have borne witness. It is important for individuals and congregations to set goals for evangelism and to rejoice when those goals are met, but we can never let *our* goals and *our* methods override the freedom of the Holy Spirit to "blow where it wills."

It is not possible to predict how the Word will work or to measure numerically the Spirit's successes. When a congregation announces its goal of fifty new members in the coming year, it appears to be most interested in "scalps" or statistics. This is the impression I get, at any rate, when I see advertisements like this:

Last Week's Sunday School Attendance: 294
Help Us Make 300!
Free T-Shirts to Every New Child
See What the Spirit Is Doing for Glad Tidings Church!

One man in my town promised to swallow a live goldfish in the pulpit if 500 people would attend services the following Sunday! Behind the hoopla, statistics, and self-congratulatory advertisements there may be some aspects of a sound theology of the cross and resurrection as well as a biblical idea of worship and discipleship, but I doubt it. In fact, the more loudly the congregation publicizes the Spirit's successes on its behalf, the more I am tempted to believe that it has lost hold of the real miracle of the Word of God. By grace we are allowed to *participate* in that Word not as promoters of ourselves but as stewards of the mysteries of God.

PRAYER

In the Word and the sacraments, God addresses us, calling us to be his own and to live under him in his kingdom. Prayer is the heart's first reply, one that is made on the most basic level imaginable. It is the birth of prayer that George Herbert describes in the resolution of his poem "The Collar":

But as I rav'd and grew more fierce and wilde
  At every word,
Me thoughts I heard one calling, *Childe:*
  And I reply'd, *My Lord.*[6]

Once the creature answers the Creator, dialogue begins in earnest. The prayerful dialogue, in which two beings are radically open and accessible to one another, supplies the *empowerment,* the *preparation,* and the *pattern* for the communication of the gospel.

The *power* of prayer lies not in our fervor, but in God's faithfulness to the divine promises. Just as we cannot predict the workings of God's proclaimed Word, so we cannot determine the mode of divine faithfulness. Two generations ago, Christian pastors, doctors, nurses, and support personnel labored in the mission fields of what was then French West Africa. They dedicated their lives to building simple hospitals and places of worship. They canoed from village to village, contracted malaria and the usual tropical diseases, and through it all prayed mightily for the outpouring of the Spirit on their endeavors. Many died before seeing many mighty works of God or anything resembling success as the world measures it. But the seed continued to grow in secret, and the prayers of these righteous men and women availed before God. Today there are more African Christians than North American Christians, and the Christian faith is finding greater acceptance on the African continent than anyplace in the world. Can we, the evangelists of our generation, pray with such a depth of faith that we are willing to forgo instant gratification and allow our children to be the harvesters of the promises and the beneficiaries of our prayers?

Such faith recognizes the principle of *preparation* at work in the communication of the gospel. The seeds of that preparation are sown in the childlike responsiveness that continually answers "My Lord" to every summons and in every crisis. The preparation matures in a life of prayer in which dialogue with God loses the quality of desperation that marks so much of our praying. Finally, preparation ripens immediately before the Christian communicator tells the story, as he or she prays that those who hear it will receive it in faith. Is not this the most mature of all the forms of prayer: the self-forgetting prayer for the other?

Preparation also means being ready for the answer that threatens to shatter our belief in prayer. Jesus prepared for the important events in his ministry—his baptism, the choosing of the Twelve, the transfiguration, and his death—by secluding himself with his Father in prayer. The answer he received was a cross, which he accepted not as the treasure he had hoped for but as the will of his Father. Our prayer too will draw us into closer fellowship with the cross and prepare us to hear and accept the will of God.

The life of prayer, then, unfolds itself as a *pattern* for a life of witness. This twofold life is open, responsive, unselfish, and accepting of another's will. Like prayer, Christian witness is willing to speak, but also to wait, to suffer, to hear, and to speak again, always secure in the assurance that these words and groanings are not the noisy static of humanity talking to itself but a participation in the ongoing dialogue with God. And when in hurt and fear the words dry up, then the dialogue gets down to basics, and the Holy Spirit prays for us "with sighs too deep for words" (Rom. 8:26). Thus prayer provides a pattern for the ultimate situation in communication, when beings dispense with that which they had relied on for communication, their precious words, and ineffably touch one another from depth to depth.

As the empowerment, the preparation, and the pattern for witness, prayer is the articulated and sometimes tongue-tied response to the goodness of God in Jesus. If the evangelist has read or listened to God's Word, he or she should pray about the content of the section just heard, thanking God for the goodness, power, and wisdom revealed in it. Second, he or she should then pray for others, especially those to whom he or she has borne witness, naming them and lifting up their needs before God. Third, the evangelist prays for radical change—that he or she might become more faithful and courageous in witnessing, and that those who hear might become doers of the Word. Fourth, if the church understands itself as evangelist to the community, the whole congregation must pray for those individuals who carry out its mission. Thus the whole witnessing enterprise advances in the context of prayer. The evangelist's lines of communication with the source of all strength and expression are never severed.

PRAYER FOR THOSE WHO SPEAK OF JESUS

O gracious God, whose Word is the source of all speech, touch the tongues and open the lips of those who would speak in your name. Where your people are ambivalent toward you and plagued with doubt, give single-minded faith; where they are inarticulate and unable to form the words, fill them with spontaneous expression; where ridicule and persecution have made them afraid, increase their courage; where the structures of unbelief around them have isolated your people from one another, open their eyes to the great cloud of witnesses and the living tradition of which they are a part. By the power of your Holy Spirit call all things to their remembrance and, in all times and all places, O Holy God, be thou the great Evangelist of your people. In the name of Jesus. Amen.

PRAYER FOR THOSE WHO HEAR

Holy Spirit of Truth, who once brooded over the face of the deep, to whom no creature is alien and no searcher hopelessly lost, prepare the hearts of those who hear your Word, that they may receive it in faith, turn from their rebellion, and come to know you as their God and Counselor. May their reunion with you then bear fruit in works of obedience, love, mercy, and justice, to the end that the church may see their lives of discipleship and give glory to you, who with the Father and the Son reigns forever and ever. Amen.

THE HOLY SPIRIT OF TRUTH

There is a prayer that Jesus encourages us to pray without reservation or qualification. It is one to which God always says yes. Comparing the heavenly Father to earthly parents (who often give their children everything they want and nothing they need), Jesus says, "how much more will the heavenly Father give the Holy Spirit to those who ask him?" (Luke 11:13).

From the beginning it was the will of Jesus that his followers have the Spirit.

"And I will pray the Father, and he will give you another Counselor, to be with you for ever, even the Spirit of truth, whom the world cannot receive, because it neither sees him or knows him; you know him, for he dwells with you, and will be in you. I will not leave you desolate; I will come to you." (John 14:16–18)

What will this new Counselor do? "But the Counselor, the Holy Spirit, whom the Father will send in my name, he will teach you all things, and bring to your remembrance all that I have said to you" (John 14:26).

John calls the Spirit "Paraclete," which is variously translated Helper, Advocate, Comforter, and Counselor. It means literally "one who is called to the side of another." In human affairs the title "counselor" is an honorable one. A counselor helps others to see the truth, to articulate it, and to act upon it. As one psychologist reminds us, "The counselor stands for reality." A psychiatric counselor is not satisifed if his or her client presents a textbook self-diagnosis ("I'm obviously suffering from an acute anxiety neurosis"), but proceeds to live an unchanged life. Nor is a pastoral counselor pleased to hear the parishioner's self-evaluation ("I'm nothing but a poor, sinful human being") without seeing the radical transformation called repentance to which this orthodox diagnosis is meant to lead. The Holy Counselor is the catalyst for change, who leads us into the truth about ourselves and God.

Most important to our purpose, the Holy Spirit enables us to witness to Christ. Michael Green points out that every initiative in evangelism recorded in Acts—Pentecost, Peter before the Sanhedrin, Stephen in Jerusalem, Philip with the eunuch, the missions of Paul—is the initiative of the Holy Spirit.[7] Even on the interpersonal level, Paul assures us that "no one can say 'Jesus is Lord' except by the Holy Spirit" (1 Cor. 12:3). A woman once chided me and the congregation I served, claiming that the Holy Spirit was not present among us. "Why do you say that?" I asked. She replied, "Because when you pray, you do not lift up your arms, and when you sing, you all have sour looks on your faces." She may have been right on both counts. But all the gifts, graces, fruits, and evidences of the Spirit are secondary in relation to this miraculous gift, the gift of articulated faith.

To Moses God promised, "I will be with your mouth." To Jeremiah the Lord said, "Behold, I have put my words in your mouth." To disciples under the pressure of persecution Jesus said, "When they deliver you up, do not be anxious how you are to speak or what you are to say; for what you are to say will be given to you in that hour; for it is not you who speak, but the Spirit of your Father speaking through you" (Matt. 10:19–20). And what does God say today to those who wish to share the Word? Has God withdrawn the promise of the Spirit? Or is it reserved only for those who testify before kings (and on television)?

In response, one might make a dogmatic defense of the abiding influence of the Holy Spirit, but given God's evangelistic purpose in sending the Spirit, I believe personal testimony is more appropriate. I can only say that the promise of the Holy Spirit means that whenever I attempt to share my faith, whether across a kitchen table with a friend or in a lecture hall, I am not alone. Our generation has heard so much about anxiety, alienation, and the plight of "modern humanity" that even Christians have begun to seek shelter in islands of personal salvation, secure from the hopeless predicament of the society around them. The Holy Spirit assures me that the kingdom of God can continue to thrive, albeit in a form I had never imagined, in a secular society and a post-Christian age. The Spirit beckons me to speak and live in the Word of Christ and rebukes me and others like me who have lost interest in the mission of the church to those who are not "church." The Spirit's message is, "Don't be afraid to speak. You are not alone." What is called to my remembrance is not the data of faith, but the living object of faith, Jesus himself. The Spirit also reminds me of the historic appropriateness of communicating the gospel and encourages me and every would-be witness to continue in the great tradition.

NOTES

1. "And we cannot be honest unless we recognize that we have to live in the world *etsi deus non daretur* [as though there were no God]. And this is just what we do recognize—before God! God himself compels us to recognize it. So our coming of age leads us to a true recognition of our situation before God. God would have us know that we must live as men who manage our lives without him. The God who is with us is the God who forsakes us (Mark 15:34). The God who lets us live in the world without the working hypothesis of God is the God before whom we stand continually. Before God and with God we live without God. God lets himself be pushed out of the world on to the cross. He is weak and powerless in the world, and that is precisely the way, the only way, in which he is with us and helps us. Matt. 8:17 makes it quite clear that Christ helps us, not by virtue of his omnipotence, but by virtue of his weakness and suffering." Dietrich Bonhoeffer, *Letters and Papers from Prison*, ed. Eberhard Bethge (New York: Macmillan Company, 1972), pp. 360–61.

2. *Lutheran Book of Worship* (1978), Hymn 183.

3. Martin Siegel, *Amen: The Diary of Rabbi Martin Siegel*, ed. Mel Ziegler (New York: Fawcett World, 1972).

4. Fred Craddock, *The Gospels* (Nashville: Abingdon Press, 1981), p. 97.

5. I have developed this more fully in *A Theology of Preaching: The Dynamics of the Gospel* (Nashville: Abingdon Press, 1981), pp. 67–69.

6. "The Collar," in *The English Poems of George Herbert,* ed. C. A. Patrides (Totowa, N.J.: Rowman & Littlefield, 1974).

7. Michael Green, *Evangelism in the Early Church* (Grand Rapids: Wm. B. Eerdmans Publishing Co., 1970), p. 149.

CHAPTER SIX

Principles of Christian Communication

Be ready at all times to answer anyone who asks you to explain the hope you have in you, but do it with gentleness and respect.

1 Pet. 3:15–16 TEV

IN THE COURSE of an evangelism training program I visited several homes as a "silent partner" to observe and benefit from the evangelistic techniques of my "trainer." The memory of one of the calls still haunts me and continues to contribute to my skepticism of all inflexible or canned approaches to witnessing. Our visit was with an elderly woman, recently widowed, who appeared so grateful for visitors that she was willing to enter into any kind of conversational arrangement. She was obviously lonely and grieving, and wept freely as she gave the "correct" responses to each of the programmed questions. After she had made the requisite commitment to Christ, she interrupted her breathless interrogator with a wry observation. "Young man, you certainly have this down pat." She would have liked to talk about her husband or her feelings of loneliness, but because the training manual suggested that the visitors vacate the premises as soon as possible after the commitment to Christ is made, the trainer whisked us out of the house, leaving me and the woman disappointed and let down.

Our calling is to communicate Christ, and that is not done by manipulating people's emotions or eliciting responses according to a planned program. That we need a simple outline or a well-internalized story is evident from the great sermons in the book of Acts, though our methodological model for witnessing need *not* be the sermon. But beyond a general framework, we need the incarnate sense of *being there* and the ability to listen, which is often destroyed by overly organized or memorized presentations. The effect of the fixed approach which, incidentally, is almost always recognized by the individual as a sales technique, may be to gloss over the individuality of the other person, to treat him or her as a "prospect." In a society in which the person too often represents little more than a "case" or a "market," we need no further blunting of individuality. People still look to the church, of all institutions, as the guarantor of the value of persons.

Unfortunately, those involved in evangelism, especially in organized evangelistic efforts, often feel like salespeople who are trying to foist an unneeded product onto an unsuspecting customer. This automatic recoil from the image of the salesperson, an unfortunate reaction to be sure, probably stems from the advertising industry's genius for creating needs for useless products. After all, who taught us to *need* 300-horsepower cars, leaf mulchers, automatic ice makers, family rooms, electric toothbrushes, and button-down collar shirts? I have had unscrupulous life insurance salespeople (*not* representative of the profession as a whole) remind me of my own mortality in order to make a sale, painting in vivid detail the conditions surrounding my unexpected demise. When I have objected to these tactics, more than one has said with a wink, "After all, we're both in the same business." No, we are not. And Paul says so:

> We are not like so many others, who handle God's message as if it were cheap merchandise; but because God has sent us, we speak with sincerity in his presence, as servants of Christ. (2 Cor. 2:17 TEV)

In the following principles of Christian communication, we shall stress the evangelist's self-understanding, his or her sensitivity to the uniqueness of other persons, and the common calling to speak of Jesus "with gentleness and respect."

BE TRUE TO YOURSELF

It is a measure of our alienation from God that we find it so difficult to communicate our faith in a congruent, natural way. If

Christian faith is an integral part of our lives, speaking of Jesus will not be an intrusion into the conversation marked by a different language and tone of voice—pious, platitudinous, pulpitish. The classic case of "pulpit tone" was that of the Rev. Mr. Sprague, described by Mark Twain in *The Adventures of Tom Sawyer*. "His voice began on a medium key and climbed steadily up till it reached a certain point, where it bore with strong emphasis upon the topmost word and then plunged down as if from a springboard:

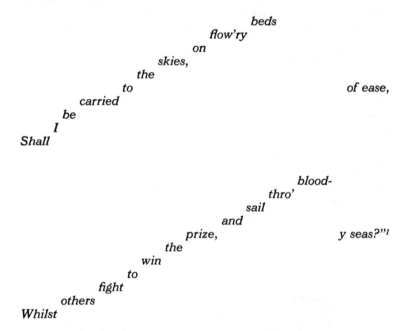

Even those who have not been to seminary or stood in a pulpit may develop a pulpit tone. The telltale changes in tone or vocabulary are signals to the listener that we have not made Christ and his gospel a part of the fabric of our lives. Instead, we have adopted a religious *persona*, thereby effectively separating the gospel from the ordinary affairs of life.

In the world of ancient Roman drama, a *persona* was a mask that enlarged and clarified the character of the dramatic figure for the sake of distant spectators. Today, *persona* continues to mean a mask, but in the opposite sense—a facade which obscures one's true identity and feelings. Everyone wears masks. The judge puts on a stern face before the sentencing; the inexperienced teacher assumes an exaggerated air of professionalism; the doctor looks calm, the lawyer cool, the mortician grave, the preacher pious. Society has persuaded itself that masks are necessary. When it comes to communication, however, the *personae* we adopt lead to superficial games between people and outright dishonesty.

Honesty begins with God or, more accurately, God's knowledge of people. Paul hoped for the day when he would understand God the way God understood him (1 Cor. 13:12). The psalmist knows that before God, who searches the heart, our masks are of no avail.

> O Lord, thou hast searched me and known me!
> Thou knowest when I sit down and when I rise up;
>   thou discernest my thoughts from afar.
> Thou searchest out my path and my lying down,
>   and art acquainted with all my ways.
> Even before a word is on my tongue, lo, O Lord,
>   thou knowest it altogether. (Ps. 139:1–4)

Knowing that *God* knows our best kept secrets, we are relieved from the burdensome task of deceiving ourselves about our feelings and motives. This means that as a young pastor I would have done well to have been honest with myself and admitted that the reason I drove up to so many strange farmhouses but never got out of the car was not my fear of farmyard dogs, but my fear of farmyard people.

To maintain an honest spirit requires self-examination. The Christian witness should do an inventory of his or her motives and feelings, asking the following kinds of questions:

Am I witnessing out of obligation?

Am I playing the numbers game on behalf of an institution?

Do I plan to manipulate the prospect into doing something?

Am I appealing to guilt, family duty, or civic respectability to persuade my neighbor to accept Christ?

Am I prepared for my neighbor's refusal or any other challenge to my values?

And as the moment of speaking draws near:

How am I feeling?
Nervous, filling with self-doubt?
Am I afraid of silence?
Do I wish I had volunteered for the Board of Properties rather
   than the work of evangelism?
Am I passing judgment on those to whom I speak?
Why is my nervousness so often tinged with anger?

WATCH YOUR LANGUAGE

As our seven-year-old son was reading the nativity story according to Luke in the Today's English Version, he stumbled over the
word "pregnant." He explained, "I didn't expect to find a word
like that in the Bible." At an early age he had already discerned
the gulf between sacred-sounding words and ordinary language.
The French missiologist Maurice Bellet calls it "split language."[2]
A confirmation student identified the problem when she asked,
"Why don't we ever hear *church words* during the week?" Why?
Because I suspect that even most Christians are uncomfortable
speaking of justification, atonement, propitiation, sanctification,
the communion of saints, and a whole company of words and
phrases that are no longer a part of most people's vocabulary and
worldview. Even if the Christian understands the meaning of
these words, it does not follow that the nonbeliever, who has rel-
egated them to that "huge dump of worn-out metaphors" (as
George Orwell described it), will benefit from a repetition of the
sacred words. Words are like the *personae* we spoke of in the previous section. They are meant to transmit meaning, but they may
effectively obliterate it.

When we speak of our faith, we do so drawing on the experience and vocabulary we have in common with others. It might
seem that after the church words are rooted out, there ought to
be many simple words, such as peace, love, and joy, whose meanings the Christian and the non-Christian share. Often, however,
the words are the same, but the meanings are different. When we
lived in England, my wife was qualified by the Educational Au-

thority to teach in the London school system. I announced to several friends that my wife had finally been certified. It took several weeks of raised eyebrows and condolences for me to discover that the usual meaning of "certified" in British English is to be declared legally insane.

It was an English writer who had one of his characters say, "When *I* use a word . . . it means just what I choose it to mean— neither more nor less."[3] To speak a word that is (1) *personal,* that is, grounded in one's own experience, (2) *faithful* to the revealed tradition, and (3) *comprehensible* to those outside the tradition is a formidable task. David Augsburger humorously illustrates the difficulty in the following exchange on the subject of conversion. *Man 2* undoubtedly knows the meaning of the individual words used by *Man 1;* what eludes him is the *meaning of the meaning.*

Man 1	Man 2
Since I got saved,	He became thrifty or religious?
I live a victorious life.	He wins all arguments.
I'm set free from sin,	He's lost interest in sex?
I've a deep settled peace,	Nothing bothers him anymore.
I never get angry and swear.	He must be lying now.
I don't smoke or drink,	No kicks.
I'm living for Jesus.	What does He have to do with this?

Is there a translator in the house?[4]

It is not enough to repeat words and phrases in the hope that they will take effect in the heart and consciousness of the unbeliever, as if by magic. It was Kierkegaard who said, "There is no lack of information in a Christian land; something else is lacking, and this is something which the one man cannot directly communicate to the other."[5] What is lacking is translation. By translation I do not mean wholesale abandonment of sacred language in favor of whatever happens to be selling well in today's marketplace. Thor Hall has exposed the silliness of religious relationships that exclude biblical talk about God. He quotes the following attempt at meaningful exchange:

> Instead of using the word "salvation," we spoke of getting to know people more deeply and getting to understand ourselves more fully. Instead of "redemption," we spoke of caring about other people,

being really concerned. Instead of "sin," we spoke of self-hate, hurt-
ing the other person, treating another person as a thing. . . . Instead
of "divine," we spoke of not knowing how to express what we feel,
of trying to reach out toward another person.[6]

This is not translation, but substitution. Translation is bipolar. It
holds onto the original words without relinquishing the demands
of the present. Translators of the gospel continue to speak the
good news, but in a tongue meaningful to its hearers. Because
sheep are all but unknown to New Guinean tribespeople, translators of the New Testament have rendered Jesus the Good
Herder of pigs. They have not eliminated Jesus or his relationship with those he loves; they have translated the message from
one idiom into another. In Chapter 3 we discussed how several
paradigms of the Christian story apply to contemporary needs.
Now Christian translators, in the neighborhoods, schools, hospitals, factories, and offices, must find the words.

LISTEN WITH YOUR WHOLE SELF

But first we listen. I can count on one hand the gifted listeners
among my friends and acquaintances. Because we have been
called to "give an account" of our hope, we have tended to neg-
lect the art of listening. A bad listener is easy to detect. His eyes
wander from yours, darting over your shoulder around the room.
Her responses are perfunctory. She asks a lot of questions and
then answers most of them herself. He never bothers to elaborate
on the stated feeling of his conversation partner. She is always
waiting for an opening to make her own point. But communication is not a game whose object is scoring points or looking for
openings. If all the evangelist can think of is "How am I going to
unload what I have to say," he or she will never hear the other
person.

A good listener uses every bodily and psychological means
available to say, "I am listening; I understand; I am right with
you." Empathy means getting into the feelings of others. It is not
the equivalent of identification, which means assuming the feelings and values of another person at the expense of one's own
identity and beliefs. Empathy facilitates communication. Identifi-

cation, because it substitutes a two-headed monologue for dialogue, makes communication impossible. In the following conversation, the first listener replies with empathy, the second with identification:

> *Elderly patient:* Another round of tests and pointless therapies. I'm nothing but a used-up consumer of medical science.
>
> *Nurse A:* You must feel like we do our jobs, but do not care enough for you.
>
> *Nurse B:* I know. Isn't it awful? This is the most impersonal place I have ever worked in.

The effective listener squares away his or her body with the other person's so that a posture of alertness and openness says, "I am paying attention to you." Do not be afraid to look at the other person. If there are two people, do not fixate on one. A good rule of thumb for the evangelist is only talk fifty percent of the time.

Nor should the evangelist fall into a pattern of questioning, as though he or she were grilling a suspect.

> *Q:* So, how long have you lived in this neighborhood?
> *A:* Six years.
> *Q:* Were you aware that Old Trinity was the nearest Presbyterian church?
> *A:* Yes, I've known about it for some time.
> *Q:* When did you first visit our worship services?
> *A:* About six weeks ago.

The question and answer format is unnatural to human conversation. If used relentlessly enough, it may produce some incriminating evidence, but little more. If questions are put, they should be used sparingly either to clear up a point of verbal misunderstanding or to help the neighbor attain greater clarity of thought. The aim of this communication is to allow the neighbor to become involved in the process of exploring the Christian faith. If questions are used, they should be as open as possible.

> You seemed very absorbed by Dr. Wilson's sermon. How would you respond to it?

> Whenever I mention the cross, I sense a feeling of apprehension. What are you thinking?

I envision the church as a servant in society; you see it as the guardian of the status quo. How can we explore that together?

How can we be sure we understand the other person? Carl Rogers's classic test of understanding continues to help communicators. "Each person can speak up for himself only *after* he has first restated the ideas and feelings of the previous speaker accurately, and to that speaker's satisfaction."[7] Although this approach has been caricatured, the evangelist can use it without himself or herself becoming a caricature of the passive counselor whose most profound contribution to dialogue consists of a litany of "uh-huhs" and "mm-hms" punctuated by excruciating silences. Evangelists should not play psychologist with people, but by their responses they can show their desire to listen and to understand.

Woman A: Sunday morning is my only chance to sleep late.
Woman B: Your job is really an exhausting one.
Man A: I read that Gospel of John you gave me. That's quite a book!
Man B: It's beginning to make sense to you.

This is not as mechanical an exercise as it sounds. The alternatives are the usual kinds of conversations that either go nowhere or escalate (or degenerate) into games of advantage. The spiral can only be halted by reflected responses from at least one of the speakers.

A second kind of response is more blatantly interpretive. After some dialogue, the evangelist is beginning to shape a feeling or an understanding of the other person.

Man A: I never get to church anymore.
Man B: Church just isn't that important to you anymore.

That is an interpretation that may or may not be accurate. It is important for the evangelist to risk careful interpretations so that, if need be, his or her thinking can be corrected and the conversation rerouted along the lines of the first speaker's intention. *Man A* may respond, "Yeah, somewhere along the way the Christian church ceased to be necessary in my life." Or he may say, "No, it's very important to me, but my arthritis has made me a prisoner in my own home." To either response the evangelist has much to offer.

A good listener manages to convey trust in the integrity and sincerity of the other person even if he or she does not agree with the other's beliefs. Our impressions and beliefs may conform to no social or historical reality, but *to us* they are supremely real. But how can misguided beliefs and mistaken impressions be real to their holder? Is not revelation clear? Is not my word good enough? And why must communication between two people be so complicated and susceptible to breakdown? In Chapters 2 and 4 we considered the spiritual reasons for our halting tongues and wooden ears.

The complexity of communication also has to do with the complexity of human beings. Modern communications theorists have diagrammed the dilemma in many ways, but I still find Oliver Wendell Holmes's explanation most congenial. In *The Autocrat of the Breakfast Table,* Holmes distinguished the following participants in a simple dialogue between John and Thomas:

1. *The real John:* known only to his Maker.
2. *John's ideal John:* never the real one, and often very unlike him.
3. *Thomas's ideal John:* never the real John, nor John's John, but often very unlike either.
4. *The real Thomas.*
5. *Thomas's ideal Thomas.*
6. *John's ideal Thomas.*

Holmes points out that we converse not merely with other persons, but with our *impressions* of others. Moreover, we communicate on the basis of firmly held but almost always mistaken impressions of ourselves. Holmes concludes, "No wonder two disputants often get angry, when there are six of them talking and listening all at the same time."[8]

The practical implications for the communication of the gospel are not difficult to discern. Any pride we take in our ability to size up other people will be dampened by our own imperfect self-knowledge. The assurance with which we shoot down the objections and disavowals of non-Christians will be tempered by a growing awareness of this six-handed poker game called dialogue. While the objections and excuses may be invalid on the basis of God's Word, their invalidity makes them no less real to the non-Christian. When your neighbor tells you that his or her disinterest in church (translate "Christ") derives from his or her parents' fanaticism ("They crammed religion down my throat"), you must know that to this person this reason for not worshiping God is a real and valid objection. Or when the shop foreman casually explains his unbelief with the words, "The church is full of hypocrites," he believes that it really is, and for him that closes the case.

Unbelief is not so simply described as the rejection of God's objectively true revelation. For human experience gives life to all sorts of impressions, ideals, beliefs, and philosophies, many of which argue against the existence of God and the work of Christ. But the same human experience with its native hope and drive toward meaning creates an immense need for the gospel of Jesus Christ. Your neighbor is not your enemy waiting to trip you up, but your brother or sister given to you by God for the purpose of glorifying God's name. And one of the first questions this neighbor asks is, "Is anyone listening to me?"

SAY IT WITH LOVE

In his important book, *The Helping Interview,* Alfred Benjamin writes, "A genuine liking for people is a gift from heaven."[9] Some textbooks call it respect or regard, others an attitude of acceptance. The Christian calls it love. Before we jump to a theological description of *agape,* self-giving love, we ought to linger over Benjamin's observation. What does it mean to have a genuine liking for people? And why is it so important for the evangelist? I suspect that a liking for people is not one of those qualities that can be successfully learned, imitated, or cultivated. It exists wherever people find the company of other human beings enjoyable and the stories of their lives interesting. Those who enjoy others are not so preoccupied with themselves that they fail to enter into the feelings of others. They do not cultivate relationships only on the basis of short-term utility or long-range potential. Those who care about others do not project genuineness as a tactic or a ploy. Their first questions upon encountering another person are not "What does she think of me?" or "What can he do for me?" but "Who are you?" "How do you think?" "What do you seek?" Those with a liking for people know that our fullest humanity is realized in the *intersection* with others. They agree with the old German maxim, *Ein Mensch ist kein Mensch,* which is to say, the individual person isolated from the community is no person at all. God has given many gifts for work in the church, but perhaps none is more necessary to the communicating of the gospel than the enjoyment of other human beings.

Perhaps this is why I have become impatient with the theorists who attempt to portray human communication by means of models originally developed at the Bell System Laboratories. The model may be as simple as $\boxed{S} \rightarrow \boxed{M} \rightarrow \boxed{R}$ or as complex as

$$\boxed{S} \rightarrow \boxed{M} \rightarrow \boxed{C} \rightarrow \boxed{R} \rightarrow \boxed{D}$$
$$\uparrow$$
$$\boxed{N}$$

In either case the warmth and vitality as well as the unpredictability of people who love other people cannot be included in the diagram. We may speak in terms of source (S), message (M), channel (C), receiver (R), destination (D), and so on, and we may even use the insulting term noise (N) to denote the genuine objections to and cultural interferences with the gospel. But without the mercurial human element, the scientific-looking communications models yield only the kind of information our common sense could have provided at half the price. More than a century ago the great Boston preacher Phillips Brooks spoke of "truth through personality" as a paradigm for the communication of the gospel. There is more to the process, to be sure, than Brooks's slogan. But today, as at no other time, his insight has become an essential corrective to all impersonal (and therefore depersonalizing) models of communication.

Communications models usually maintain a clear distinction between the source of a message and its receiver. A Christian the-

ology of communication also retains the separateness of evangelist and nonbeliever. Christian love is not afraid to be other than
and different from those to whom it is offered. But here the mystery of Christian love becomes more intense. The Christ who
both empowers us to love and is the content of our message now
appears in the confused, indifferent, or antagonistic *other*. The
neighbor becomes, as Luther said, a "little Christ to me" and is
respected and loved as such. This realization marks the end of
the evangelistic siege mentality that pits "us" against "them," for
the same Christ-in-me now stands before me as Christ-in-
neighbor.

TELL YOUR STORY

After the listening and the interpretive reflection, there is a time
to speak; there is a time to tell your story. It is not a monologue
designed to cap off the conversation, but it is a coherent narrative
which, one hopes, will answer the proverb,

> A word fitly spoken
> is like apples of gold in a setting of silver. (Prov. 25:11)

During a retreat on evangelism after I had outlined the narrative shape of God's revelation to Israel and the church (see Chapter 3), an impatient participant interrupted me and said, "That's
all very interesting; but if a non-Christian were to ask me to explain my faith, I wouldn't know where to begin. What do I say,
'In the beginning God created the heavens and the earth' and
take it from there? How would *you* start?" He might have added,
"And what if you have no dramatic conversion story to tell?"
What if you have not been a prodigal son or daughter and come
to your senses in the pigsty of a bar on Highway 40 or the squalor
of a divorce court or in the far country of suburban materialism
and malaise? Does this absence of the sensational mean you have
no story to tell? I could only respond by telling my story.

"My faith was given to me as a gift. Although I have come to
understand it as a gift from God, its first givers in my experience
were my parents. The whole gift nature of life in Christ is what
Christians mean by grace. I never had a cataclysmic religious ex-

perience that changed my life-style, but through years of nurture in a Christian family and in a Christian congregation, my belief in Christ was formed, shaped, and fed—indeed, so thoroughly molded that I have a difficult time imagining myself outside Christ. The older I get the more I appreciate this gift nature of faith and, therefore, the more I give thanks for Christian parents. And the more I wonder at the miracle of baptism.

"I was adopted by God in my baptism. I had not reached the age of reason or spiritual sensitivity; but God took the initiative and moved toward me as a would-be parent reaches out in love toward a foundling. In the waters of baptism God washed me clean of the terminal spiritual illness with which and in which I was born, and made me God's own child. In the words that were spoken in the water, God promised to be my God forever. The God of Abraham, Isaac, Jacob, and Jesus was now my God and Father. In my baptism I became a member of Christ's body, the church. It means a lot to me that when the promises of God were read and the water was applied, the whole congregation along with my parents and grandparents said, 'Amen!'

"Whatever spiritual growth and renewal I have experienced has been a kind of explication or living out of this baptism. When my parents told the Bible stories, enrolled me in Sunday school, and taught me to pray, they were activating my baptism and making it work in my life. For at the baptismal font God was not the only one who made promises. My parents also promised to pray for me, teach me the Ten Commandments, the Creeds, the Lord's Prayer, the stories of the Scripture, and to lead me into a life of worship. I am telling you all this only to help you see this envelope of God's grace in which I live. It may sound to you like my faith is a thing of the past. It's not. I'm just talking about my roots. If the principles by which you live are not rooted in God's grace, you won't know who you are or what you believe.

"When you ask me 'When were you *saved?*' I can only point to an occurrence in history that happened long before I was born— the crucifixion and resurrection of Christ. This was God's action in Christ to reconcile the whole world. There is nothing I see in humanity that wants to love God. Oh, there is a shadowy knowledge, a 'somebody up there' kind of thing, and there is an innate curiosity about God, weaker in some, stronger in others. But there is no natural drive to love or serve God. And as the Bible and history testify, there is no natural drive in us to love one another. The anxiety, hatred, separation, uneasy conscience, fear of death, and all the rest of it, God takes on in Jesus Christ. Jesus becomes a brother to us in order to make us children of God. Now, when you ask, 'When were *you* saved?' I must again point to my baptism. For that was God's personal covenant with me, when I received the benefits of Christ's life, death, and resurrection.

"Certainly, I've had my share of times when I've either been having too good a time to remember God or been so hurt and disappointed that I have shaken my fist at God and ordered my Creator out of my life. At times like that my life has been as empty as a vacant house, as dead as a corpse. During those periods I have lived as though I had never had Christian parents, been baptized, or known Jesus in any way. In all honesty I could say with Peter, 'I do not know the man,' and by my behavior no one would have ever guessed the truth. It's a terrible power we have, this veto we may exercise over baptism and God's grace. It's *terrible* because we do it with such callousness and efficiency, and *powerful* because it effectively cuts us off from the Father and our spiritual home. I suspect you have endured this separation too. Where are these dry places? We all have different spiritual maps. I have come upon them in times of loneliness and also in moments of professional success. That's when I feel most susceptible to despair or self-sufficiency. How is it with you?

"When renewal comes, as it always does, I experience it as something old and something new. Old: it is a remembering of God's covenant. New: God's grace always startles me with its power to energize and create new possibilities. It invariably happens in community with other Christians—through worship and acts of faithfulness toward others. Worship and discipleship both help me become less preoccupied with my self and my self's problems and more open to the needs of others. Praise of God in worship and service to others in love turns us inside out and reminds us of responsibilities greater than the maintenance of our own egos. This renewed energy we experience is the work of God the Holy Spirit.

"The Spirit is not bound to any set pattern of change. You do not have to have an acceptable history for the Spirit to work with. Nor must you come from good Christian stock or have the requisite educational background to qualify for membership in the Christian church. You will need only to sense that your story is somehow incomplete or broken, that you have not lived it according to God's original design. By God's grace, the Spirit works this transformation called repentance and faith. God calls you, as God continually calls me, to a new life. What is your response to this?"

Telling any story, especially one that is filtered through one's own experience, comes with built-in limitations and dangers. *Any* story, no matter how simple and "artless" its plot and characterization, is an aesthetic artifact that necessarily limits its audience. Its language, plot, and structure include some listeners and exclude others. Considering the above testimonial, for instance, some people may not understand a sacramental approach to Christian living or may not identify with a faith that has roots in the actions of parents and grandparents. In other words, your story may set you apart from your neighbor; it may be heard as something peculiarly and inimitably *yours*.

The danger of storytelling, of course, lies in our own tendency toward self-centeredness. Instead of being a vehicle of God's grace, my story may remain transparent to the needs of my ego but opaque to the demands of God. The *"me* decades" of the seventies and eighties have discovered the joys of "getting my head together," "doing my own thing" ("I did it my way"), "getting in touch with myself," and "getting myself saved." What could be more natural (and more accommodating) to a narcissistic culture than a form of evangelism in which I am encouraged to talk about my favorite subject, namely, *me*! If evangelism as storytelling never rises above specialization in the self, it will hug the earth like a deflated balloon and fail its high calling of God. If we are preoccupied with earthly matters, how shall we ascend to the divine? (See John 3:12.)

Yet there it is, three times in the book of Acts: Paul's story. "As

I made my journey and drew near to Damascus, about noon a great light from heaven suddenly shone about me. . . ." This is not the whole of Pauline theology, nor does this singular incident do justice to the full story of Paul's conversion. But without it, we would not understand Paul's witness to the gospel.

I should like to conclude this chapter by offering excerpts from the stories of five Christians: an ancient Father of the church, two Protestant Reformers, and two modern Catholics. In no case do these statements represent the totality of the narrator's spiritual journey. They are only fragments of what for each of the five was a long process of conversion.

Augustine: I went to Carthage, where I found myself in the midst of a hissing cauldron of lust. I had not yet fallen in love, but I was in love with the idea of it, and this feeling that something was missing made me despise myself for not being more anxious to satisfy the need. I began to look around for some object for my love, since I badly wanted to love something. I had no liking for the safe path without pitfalls, for although my real need was for you, my God, who are the food of the soul, I was not aware of this hunger.[10]

Luther: Though I lived as a monk without reproach, I felt that I was a sinner before God with an extremely disturbed conscience. I could not believe that he was placated by my satisfaction. I did not love, yes, I hated the righteous God who punishes sinners, and secretly, if not blasphemously, certainly murmuring greatly, I was angry with God. . . . Thus I raged with a fierce and troubled conscience. Nevertheless, I beat importunately upon Paul at that place, most ardently desiring to know what St. Paul wanted. At last, by the mercy of God, meditating day and night, I gave heed to the context of the words, namely, "In it the righteousness of God is revealed, and it is written, 'He who through faith is righteous shall live.' " There I began to understand that the righteousness of God is that by which the righteous lives by a gift of God, namely by faith. . . . Here I felt that I was altogether born again and had entered paradise itself through open gates.[11]

Wesley: In the evening I went very unwillingly to a society in Aldersgate Street, where one was reading Luther's preface to the *Epistle to the Romans*. About a quarter before nine, while he was describing the change which God works in the heart through faith in Christ, I felt my heart strangely warmed. I felt I did trust in Christ, Christ alone for salvation; and an assurance was given me that he had taken away *my* sins, even *mine,* and saved *me* from the law of sin and death.[12]

Merton: Such was the death of the hero, the great man I had wanted to be. Externally (I thought) I was a big success. Everybody knew who I was at Columbia. Those who had not yet found out, soon did when the Yearbook came out, full of pictures of myself. . . . They did not have to be very acute to see through the dumb self-satisfied expression in all those portraits. The only thing that surprises me is that no one openly reproached or mocked me for such ignominious vanity. No one threw any eggs at me, nobody said a word. . . . The wounds within me were, I suppose, enough. I was bleeding to death. . . . I had come very far, to find myself in this blind-alley: but the very anguish and helplessness of my position was something to which I rapidly succumbed. And it was my defeat that was to be the occasion of my rescue.[13]

Day: I was surprised that I found myself beginning to pray daily. I could not get down on my knees, but I could pray while I was walking. If I got down on my knees I thought, "Do I really believe? Whom am I praying to?" A terrible doubt came over me, and a sense of shame, and I wondered if I was praying because I was lonely, because I was unhappy. . . . "But," I reasoned with myself, "I am praying because I am happy, not because I am unhappy. I did not turn to God in unhappiness, in grief, in despair—to get consolation, to get something from Him." And encouraged that I was praying because I wanted to thank Him, I went on praying. No matter how dull the day, how long the walk seemed, if I felt sluggish at the beginning of the walk, the words I had been saying insinuated themselves into my heart before I had finished, so that on the trip back I neither prayed nor thought but was filled with exultation.[14]

Now, what's your story? Are you ready to tell it?

NOTES

1. Mark Twain, *The Adventures of Tom Sawyer* (New York: New American Library, n.d.), p. 39.

2. Maurice Bellet, *Facing the Unbeliever,* trans. Eva Fleischner (New York: Herder and Herder, 1967), p. 138.

3. Lewis Carroll, *Through the Looking Glass* (San Rafael, Calif.: Classic Publishing Corporation, 1970), p. 143.

4. David W. Augsburger, *Communicating Good News* (Scottdale, Pa.: Herald Press, 1972), p. 33.

5. Fred B. Craddock has written a book-length commentary on this sentence. See his *Overhearing the Gospel* (Nashville: Abingdon Press, 1978).

6. William L. Malcomson quoted in Thor Hall, *The Future Shape of Preaching* (Philadelphia: Fortress Press, 1971), p. 84.

7. Carl Rogers, *On Becoming a Person* (Boston: Houghton Mifflin, 1961), p. 332.

8. Oliver Wendell Holmes, *The Autocrat of the Breakfast Table* (New York: Thomas Y. Crowell & Co., 1900), pp. 50–51. Holmes adds that immediately after he offered this analysis a young man named John, sitting beside him at table, promptly devoured the remaining three peaches in the basket before him "remarking that there was just one apiece for him" (p. 52).

9. Alfred Benjamin, *The Helping Interview*, 2d ed. (Boston: Houghton Mifflin, 1974), p. 41.

10. Augustine, *Confessions* III. i.

11. "Preface to the Complete Edition of Luther's Latin Writings, 1545," *Martin Luther, Selections from his Writings*, ed. John Dillenberger (Garden City, N.Y.: Doubleday & Co., 1961), p. 11.

12. *The Journal of the Rev. John Wesley, A.M.*, vol. I, ed. Nehemiah Curnock (London: The Epworth Press, 1938), pp. 475–76.

13. Thomas Merton, *The Seven Storey Mountain* (New York: Harcourt Brace Jovanovich, 1976), pp. 164–65.

14. Dorothy Day, *The Long Loneliness* (New York: Harper & Brothers, 1952), pp. 132–33, paragraphing altered.

CHAPTER SEVEN

Strategies

To the weak I became weak, that I might win the weak. I have become all things to all men, that I might by all means save some.

1 Cor. 9:22

It is time to begin. You already sensed that when you chose to read this book. The concluding chapter will draw together many of the themes of the book and suggest strategies for beginning the long-deferred work of communicating the gospel.

PERSONAL

Do a spiritual history of your development in faith. Depending on your theological stance, the history may begin with baptism or a conversion experience and proceed to follow an irregular pattern of depressions and spurts of growth. Most of us know where we have been financially and educationally; we can trace progress or the lack of it in business or other professional endeavors. But when it comes to our life with God in the church, we have given little consideration to spiritual development and have never tried to measure or chart it. If my salary were the same as it was ten years ago, I would be concerned; yet when my prayer life, knowledge of the Bible, or everyday Christian discipline remains at "preinflationary" levels, that is, if I am spiritually about the same as I always had been, I maintain a remarkable calm. Measuring faith development means asking questions like: How have I grown in grace? How and where has Christ's gospel held me in good stead? What has life been like when I relied on resources other than God?

109

Make a commitment to spiritual discipline. There are many forms of discipline. Let us consider four that are basic to any effort at spiritual growth: Word, sacrament, prayer, and service. Make a commitment to read the word of God devotionally, meditatively, so that its central message begins to speak directly to you. Attend the Holy Communion regularly, every time it is offered. This, of course, entails worship, but the *koinonia* or fellowship one experiences in the sacrament is at the deepest level a meeting with the risen Christ. Choose three times a day for prayer and then devote yourself—all your physical and mental powers—to prayer, especially for those to whom you will bear witness (see Chapter 5). Look for opportunities for Christian service to those in need. I say "service" instead of "love" because we are aiming at something greater than a feeling or a quality, something the Bible calls *diakonia*, literally "waiting at tables." Find a way to *help* those to whom you would communicate Christ.

Prepare your message. Paul never hesitated to speak of "my gospel." By this he did not mean a message distorted by his own idiosyncracies, but an unchanging gospel given the stamp of his authority and experience. So this gospel we prepare is *ours*. No one can tell the gospel exactly the way I do. The shape of your gospel will be determined by three factors. The most important, of course, is the word of God—the message of Christ's cross and resurrection. The second factor is your own story. How one has experienced the gospel must influence the way it is shared with others. The third factor is the personality or situation of the one to whom the gospel is addressed. Within the bounds of biblical doctrine, the situation of the unbeliever will elicit a gospel presentation shaped to specific needs. Earlier chapters have addressed these three factors in some detail. The evangelist studies the Word, assesses his or her own experience of the good news, listens carefully and diagnostically to the needs of the non-Christian, and at the right time and right place brings the Christian gospel to expression. The evangelist must take whatever steps are necessary to insure that he or she is equipped for this work of ministry. This equipping may take the form of intensive training and practice sponsored by the local congregation.

Use the Bible and other literature of the church in the act of communicating the faith. I am a great believer in giving the Bible, or portions of it, to those who are ready to read it. Such a gift is a loving gesture with a substantial impact. It is something you and your friend can return to again and again. The American Bible Society publishes individual books of the New Testament in inexpensive paperback editions (for example, *Good News by a Man Named John*) that are less forbidding than a complete King James Version of the Bible. The evangelist may mark passages or sections of the Scripture that summarize the story of salvation or represent a congregation's understanding of ministry. One group of Christians I know buys inexpensive copies of John's Gospel and marks them according to its members' understanding of the good news and the role of the church in the community. The passages marked are John 3:16–17, the loving initiative of God in Christ; John 11:25–26, Christ's power over death; John 13:34–35, love for one another—the mark of discipleship; John 17:21, the unity of God's people; John 20:30–31, the purpose of this Gospel. This in no way replaces the give and take, listening, telling, and doing that is evangelism, but it is one way of giving a tangible gift and, with it, the greater gift.

When it comes to secondary Christian literature, the evangelist must be sensitive to the tastes and capabilities of his or her neighbor. The author of the recommended book is in a sense being enlisted by you, the evangelist, to help in the work of gospel communication. Depending on the recipient's literary tastes and interests, the gift may range from Augustine's *Confessions* or Bunyan's *Pilgrim's Progress* to C. S. Lewis's *Mere Christianity,* from Bonhoeffer's *Life Together* to Teilhard de Chardin's *How I Believe,* or from Dorothy Day's *The Long Loneliness* to Keith Miller's *The Taste of New Wine* or Eldridge Cleaver's *Soul on Ice.* Whatever the book, it is never enough to give it without commenting on the book's importance or appeal. Secondary Christian literature as a witnessing aid cannot take the place of one person at the side of another.

SOCIAL

Do an inventory of your relatives, friends, and neighbors who are not Christian. By now the statistics have become so familiar that no one need stereotype evangelism as an abrasive encounter between strangers. A recent Gallup survey reports that fifty-seven percent of those who attend church regularly first began because they were invited by someone they knew. Lyle Schaller has found that between two-thirds and three-fourths of the church members he surveyed came to the church through friendship or kinship ties.[1] Before we look to a field outside the realm of our experience, we need to survey the people God has put in our path with whom we might develop a deeper relationship. Think of the next door neighbor without a church, the occasional tennis partner, the secretary or business associate we see at coffee break, Aunt Dorothy and Uncle Ed who gave up on the Methodists ten years ago, the child for whom church attendance has become a matter of coercion. One observer of the contemporary church has come to the realization "that many of us active American churchmen are stumbling over the bodies of our wives and children and people in our daily paths in order to participate in time-consuming, promoted evangelistic programs."[2] We will never fully appreciate the accuracy of that observation until we actually list these people God has already given us and make them the primary objects of our prayer and witness.

Cultivate non-Christian acquaintances. Our first inclination is to associate with our own kind: bricklayers with bricklayers, singles with singles, stockbrokers with stockbrokers, housewives with housewives, teachers with teachers, and, the previous paragraph notwithstanding, Christians with Christians. Christians have long counseled one another to build and maintain relationships within the body of Christ, the church. So most congregations not only promote fellowship in Word and sacrament, which is the source and core of true *koinonia,* but they also sponsor young adult picnics, women's bowling leagues, and teen coffeehouses, all on the assumption that Christians ought to rub shoulders with other Christians. Why? There may be sound theological reasons behind the assumptions, but more often there are other, less attractive motives behind so-called Christian fellowship. One is convenience: it is simply inconvenient to venture out of one's spiritual enclave to relate to those who think another way. Dialogue is hard work. A second motive is fear. We remain in our religious ghetto for fear of being corrupted or persuaded by the life style or arguments of the non-Christian. Yet if the Christian enjoys the primary fellowship of the church and its nurture, he or she has nothing to fear from the cultivation of relationships with non-Christians. How else will the evangelist ever be in a position to make a personal, in-depth presentation of the gospel? Paul clears up a misunderstanding among his congregation when he explains, "When I wrote in my letter to you not to associate with people living immoral lives, I was not meaning to include all the people in the world who are sexually immoral, any more than I meant to include all usurers and swindlers or idol worshippers. To do that, you would have to withdraw from the world altogether. What I wrote was that you should not associate with a brother Christian who is leading an immoral life . . . (1 Cor. 5:9–11 JB).

Work with non-Christians in service projects. The best place to begin the relationship is on common ground where Christian and non-Christian share a concern and even a passion for helping others. Historically, the Christian church has suffered severe spells of *integralism,* which is the requirement of total doctrinal agreement as a prerequisite for social or political cooperation. A classic example of the breaking down of integralism occurred during the 1968 Soviet invasion of Czechoslovakia when Christians and communists, who had worked together for political reforms, joined in the denunciation of the invasion. Another instance occurred during the years of America's involvement in Vietnam when an antiwar coalition of Christian and various non-Christian activist groups joined to form the peace movement. On the community level, it may be an effort to establish a halfway house for runaways, a voter registration drive, or a movement to clean up the local landfill; whatever the project, it provides an arena for cooperation in which Christians and their brothers and sisters outside the church may see one another at their best. For the Christian such experiences are reminders of the aspirations common to all humanity; for the non-Christian they witness to the church's this-worldly concern and shatter the stereotype of Christianity as a Sunday morning religion.

CONGREGATIONAL

This book has aimed at equipping persons to share their faith. Since it is not a manual for congregational growth, it would be inappropriate to offer here in abbreviated form prescriptions for church organization and growth that are available in many books (see the reading list at the end of this book). Nor is it my intention to become embroiled in an assessment and critique of the church growth movement that has swept across American Protestantism. I think it best to limit my discussion of congregational strategies to the lay Christian's relationship to his or her congregation and the role the evangelist can play in equipping the congregation (it is usually vice versa) for the work of evangelism.

Alert the congregation to the importance of evangelism. In the average congregation the pastor, staff, and informed lay leadership plan programs "from on high" and proceed to recruit, train, and inspire workers from within the ranks of the membership. But there are still many congregations that do no evangelism, and I am meeting increasing numbers of individuals who have experienced the joy of communicating the faith and now want to inspire and influence their congregation to make evangelism a part of its intentional ministry. This can be done informally at first through coffees, prayer, and study circles or other small group formats. Several individuals may covenant with one another to prepare themselves for witness, to pray for one another, and to share their faith in whatever way possible.

Later they may encourage the deacons or elders to commission a study of the immediate community to ascertain its needs. They may also *dis*courage the church leadership from trying to limit the composition of the congregation to one identifiable type of membership unit (for example, the young-to-middle-aged family) in order to maintain the rich texture of the body of Christ in which individuals of heterogeneous socioeconomic groups experience the reconciliation that is not available to them in the world. These vanguard witnesses will also propose a self-study to determine how and why people have become involved (or disinterested) in the congregation. This will entail a careful and realistic (!) review of membership statistics. And it may help do away with that bugaboo of all statistical studies, the nonresidential member.

At the same time or somewhat later, those interested in witnessing may ask the pastor or minister of education to offer evangelism workshops in a setting more formal than the small covenant and prayer groups. They may also suggest that the pastor preach a series of sermons on the communication of the gospel. It is hoped that these conversations will produce a sense of partnership between pastor and people so that minister and member will feel comfortable visiting non-Christians together and encouraging one another in witness. Many clergy need this encouragement more than the members of their churches, for most professional ministers are overscheduled as it is and may have little recent experience of the person-to-person verbalization of the gospel which, from the protected confines of the pulpit, they have frequently urged upon their people. Thus the layperson who is tuned in to evangelism may lead his or her pastor into liberating experiences of witness on the cutting edge of the church. However it happens, neither pastor nor layperson should forget that the communication of the gospel takes practice, and that means not only holding seminars about witnessing, but doing it, and more than that, doing it in the presence of a brother or sister who is supportive of the task.

Help the church assess its advertisements of itself. Many congregations have no idea of the kind of face they project into the community, while others are so preoccupied with their image that they exude superficiality. A church in our community had this sign at the corner of its property: "A Friendly Church With A Smile As Bright As Its Future." How I longed for some trustee or aggravated member to uproot that sign and to replace it with some New Testament advertising: "We Preach Christ Crucified."

The signs, of course, only symbolize the church's perception of itself and its stance in the community. A congregation's programs, budget, use of facilities, and its public proclamations are often unintentional self-advertisements and ways of saying, "This is who we are." The church of the innocuous sign may in fact preach and follow Christ crucified, only it does not have the confidence to identify itself to the community as a servant of Christ. Confusion arises, however, when the evangelist shares the gospel of the crucified Christ with a friend and then brings that friend to worship, where the visitor discovers a puzzling discrepancy between the message proclaimed by the evangelist and the image projected by the church.

Help the church examine or reexamine the quality of its Sunday morning worship. Once again, it is essential that the congregation's worship live up to the high calling of the gospel, otherwise the visitor will stumble over the discrepancy between personal message and corporate practice. Worship is or should be a celebration and an application of that gospel shared by the evangelist. Its dynamic interaction of Word and sacrament should not be flattened by a long series of clublike announcements for insiders only, nor should its focal proclamation (the sermon) decline into the minister's ramblings and private reflections. The evangelist may help his or her congregation evaluate its public worship by the only catholic and ecumenical criterion available to Christians, namely, the good news of Jesus Christ. Diagram your worship services to see where they are going in terms of the good news. What activities are invested with the most ceremonial care? If it is the offering or the snuffing of the candles, the congregation's worship may be in trouble. How discouraging it is to the evangelist to spend weeks cultivating the neighbor in order to bring him or her into the midst of the worshiping community—where nothing is happening!

Help integrate the outsider into the life of the congregation. I
once knew a young woman who regularly every Friday or Satur-
day night broke into the church to pray. Many times I offered her
a key to the building, but no, as far as she was concerned
churches are for breaking into. I never fully understood the dynamic at work in her or in the congregation that caused her to see
the church as a citadel to be stormed rather than a community to
be joined.

This true story is a kind of parable of the obstacles faced by
the outsider who must walk into the bastion of insiders. The evangelist can help sensitize the congregation to the many ways it says
KEEP OUT to the newcomer. The needlessly complicated worship folder, the lack of a nursery or other provisions for children,
the cliquish gatherings after services, the obvious social stratifi-
cations among members—these and many other indicators all
say, "Though our doors are open, we are closed to you." Those
members who are not yet ready for witnessing may be recruited
to provide a support and assimilation system for newcomers. In
the early stages of a congregation's evangelism awareness, it may
be the evangelist who provides not only a witness to Christ, but
also a practical means of entering into this sometimes impenetra-
ble complex called the church.

Of course, assimilation into the church describes more than a
process of socialization or settling into comfortable patterns of
friendship and organizational loyalties. At its most profound
level, assimilation is incorporation or *in-bodiment* into Christ
through baptism, and marks the beginning of new lives of discipleship. And in that way, the cycle of evangelism continues.

NOTES

1. Reported in McGavran and Hunter, *Church Growth: Strategies
That Work* (Nashville: Abingdon Press, 1980), pp. 33–34.
2. Keith Miller and Bruce Larson, *Living the Adventure* (Waco:
Word Books, 1975), p. 101.

For Further Reading

The following is not a comprehensive bibliography, but a personal selection of books for those who wish to do in-depth reading.

THE CASE FOR CHRISTIANITY

Chesterton, C. K. *The Everlasting Man.* Westport, Conn.: Greenwood Press, 1974.

Küng, Hans. *On Being a Christian*, trans. Edward Quinn. Garden City, N.Y.: Doubleday, 1976.

Langford, Thomas A. *Christian Wholeness.* Nashville: The Upper Room, 1978.

Lewis, C. S. *Mere Christianity.* New York: Macmillan Company, 1960.

———— *The Screwtape Letters.* Philadelphia: Fortress Press, 1980.

Muggeridge, Malcolm. *Jesus Rediscovered.* Garden City, N.Y.: Doubleday & Co., 1969.

Phillips, J. B. *God Our Contemporary.* New York: Macmillan Company, 1960.

———— *Your God Is Too Small.* New York: Macmillan Company, 1953.

Thielicke, Helmut. *How to Believe Again*, trans. H. George Anderson. Philadelphia: Fortress Press, 1972.

Weatherhead, Leslie. *A Plain Man Looks at the Cross.* Nashville: Abingdon Press, 1945.

CHURCH GROWTH

Hunter, George G. *The Contagious Congregation.* Nashville: Abingdon Press, 1979.

McGavran, Donald. *Understanding Church Growth*. Grand Rapids: Wm. B. Eerdmans Publishing Co., 1970.

McGavran, Donald and Arn, Winfield. *Ten Steps for Church Growth*. San Francisco: Harper & Row, 1977.

McGavran, George and Hunter, George G. *Church Growth: Strategies That Work*. Nashville: Abingdon Press, 1980.

COMMUNICATION

Augsburger, David W. *Communicating Good News*. Scottdale, Pa.: Herald Press, 1972.

Bellet, Maurice. *Facing the Unbeliever*, trans. Eva Fleischner. New York: Herder and Herder, 1967.

Hesselgrave, David J. *Communicating Christ Cross-culturally*. Grand Rapids: Zondervan Publishing House, 1978.

Nida, Eugene. *Message and Mission: The Communication of the Christian Faith*. New York: Harper & Brothers, 1960.

HISTORY OF EVANGELISM

Aixala, Jerome. *Witnessing and Martyrdom*. Bandra, Bombay: St. Paul Press, 1969.

Green, Michael. *Evangelism in the Early Church*. Grand Rapids: Wm. B. Eerdmans Publishing Co., 1970.

Scharpff, Paulus. *History of Evangelism*, trans. Helga Bender Henry. Grand Rapids: Wm. B. Eerdmans Publishing Co., 1966.

Simmons, Dawn Langley. *The Sawdust Trail*. Philadelphia: Macrae Smith Co., 1964.

STORIES OF FAITH

Augustine. *The Confessions*, trans. R. S. Pine-Coffin. New York: Penguin Books, 1961.

Bunyan, John. *Grace Abounding to the Chief of Sinners*. London: SCM Press, 1955.

Campbell, Will. *Brother to a Dragonfly*. New York: Seabury Press, 1979.

Day, Dorothy, *The Long Loneliness*. New York: Harper & Brothers, 1952.

Merton, Thomas. *The Seven Storey Mountain.* New York: Harcourt Brace Jovanovich, 1976.

Teresa of Avila. *The Life of Saint Teresa of Avila,* trans. J. M. Cohen. Harmondsworth, Eng.: Penguin Books, 1957.

Thurman, Howard. *With Head and Heart.* New York: Harcourt Brace Jovanovich, 1979.

THEOLOGY AND PRACTICE OF EVANGELISM

Armstrong, Richard. *Service Evangelism.* Philadelphia: Westminster Press, 1979.

Facre, Gabriel. *Do and Tell: Engagement Evangelism in the '70s.* Grand Rapids: Wm. B. Eerdmans Publishing Co., 1973.

Fisher, Wallace. *Because We Have Good News.* Nashville: Abingdon Press, 1974.

Laney, James T., ed. *Evangelism: Mandate for Action.* New York: Hawthorn Books, 1975.

Moberg, David O. *The Great Reversal: Evangelism and Social Concern,* rev. ed. Philadelphia: J. B. Lippincott Company, 1977.

Mueller, Charles S. *The Strategy of Evangelism.* St. Louis: Concordia Publishing House, 1965.

Niles, D. T. *The Message and Its Messengers.* Nashville: Abingdon Press, 1966.

———— *That They May Have Life.* New York: Harper & Brothers, 1951.

Outler, Albert. *Evangelism in the Wesleyan Spirit.* Nashville: Tidings, 1971.

Quere, Ralph W. *Evangelical Witness.* Minneapolis: Augsburg Publishing House, 1975.

Shoemaker, Samuel. *With the Holy Spirit and with Fire.* New York: Harper & Brothers, 1960.

Sweazey, George. *The Church as Evangelist.* San Francisco: Harper & Row, 1978.

Telling My Story, Sharing My Faith. Toronto: United Church of Canada, n.d.

Verney, Stephen. *Fire in Coventry.* Old Tappan, N.J.: Fleming Revell, 1964.

Westerhoff, John H. III. *Will Our Children Have Faith?* New York: Seabury Press, 1976.